The Asking Mystery

MICHAEL GELVEN

The Asking Mystery

A Philosophical Inquiry

THE PENNSYLVANIA STATE UNIVERSITY PRESS
UNIVERSITY PARK, PENNSYLVANIA

Permission to reprint the line from W. H. Auden's poem "The Sea and the Mirror" has been given by Random House Inc. from *W. H. Auden: Collected Poems*, edited by Edward Mendelson. Copyright 1940 and renewed 1968 by W. H. Auden.

Library of Congress Cataloging-in-Publication Data

Gelven, Michael.
    The asking mystery : a philosophical inquiry / by Michael Gelven.
        p.   cm.
    Includes index.
    ISBN 0-271-01985-9 (alk. paper)
    ISBN 0-271-01986-7 (pbk. : alk. paper)
    1. Inquiry (Theory of knowledge)   I. Title.
  BD183.G45   2000
  121'.6—dc21   99-29264
                                                 CIP

It is the policy of The Pennsylvania State University Press to use acid-free paper for the first printing of all clothbound books. Publications on uncoated stock satisfy the minimum requirements of American National Standard for Information Sciences—Permanence of Paper for Printed Library Materials, ANSI Z39.48–1992.

To Tom Nugent

Contents

Acknowledgments

This book was written during the released time provided by the award of a Presidential Research Professorship granted by Northern Illinois University; I am grateful for the opportunity provided by that award. Since this book is the product of much personal reflection, I also wish to express my indebtedness to those who were willing to read parts of the manuscript and to listen to my arguments. For Dr. Herman Stark especial thanks for reading it in its entirety and providing many helpful comments and critiques; also thanks to my sister Dr. Fran Mayeski, Dr. Francisco Gonzalez, my nephew Dr. Michael Degnan, and many of my students, especially Adam Biesterfeld, Chris Morgan, Tom Nugent, and Mark Hinsch. Without great students how could we possibly learn?

Introduction

It is a custom more honored in the breach than the observance.
—*Hamlet:* I. iii

All the major philosophers, both modern and classic, give lip service to the importance of questions or questioning. Such service is not unlike the jaded skeptic re-entering the temple or church, nodding to the altar; it has become a ritual, a pious propriety, or even a habit. The myriad thinkers solemnly protest their reverence for the asking sacrament; and then go on with their answering business as if the rite had not occurred at all. Yet, surely, of all the things thinkers do, asking must be ranked truly supreme, and not be merely ceremonially greeted at the doorway and then dismissed. How is it possible for us to raise questions, particularly those whose raisings seem so fundamental? What must be presupposed about us human thinkers that accounts for our asking? What does it mean for us to ask at all? The glib answer to such questioning is this: we want to know what we do not yet know; so asking is accounted for by ordinary curiosity. It does not take long to realize this account is unsatisfactory; there obviously is more to it than that.

It was with some sense of awe and bewilderment that, being puzzled by this, I looked around the various resources thinkers have at their disposal, and found—nothing. Or practically nothing. There was no major or even minor work that considered the phenomenon of asking as a topic worthy in itself of being seriously addressed. There were a few hints scattered here and there, especially in Plato and Heidegger, but nowhere was there a sustained inquiry of the sort that almost every other topic seemed to have deserved. There were some remarkably dense articles by the symbolic logicians on the purely formal relations in what is called erotetic logic; but these were of no benefit at all. And so I wrote this book.

It was something of an epiphany. The fact is, the sorry lack of ongoing or traditional literature on the topic gives this inquiry a freshness coupled with a depth of challenge that daunted as well as thrilled. I was forced to hew my own tools, as it were; cut the trail as well as follow it; and at times I confess submitting to a palpable joy at the incredible richness that seemed to be hitherto untapped. I felt a Columbus, stumbling across a new, unexpected continent. It is not, I confess, considered proper at all for a philosophical author to admit such personal reactions; but I mention them here to prepare the reader for what might seem rather unorthodox approaches in the text, both in style and content. Nor am I entirely convinced that this reluctance to include an author's reaction to a discovery does not impede rather than enhance the search for truth. Besides, what else is an introduction for?

Indeed, introductions to philosophical works are always somewhat enigmatic. To suggest the reader needs one is to confess the text itself is lacking in some way. If there is something new in the introduction, why not put it in the main body of the text? If there is nothing new, why have it at all? Indeed, introductions often tend to be reductionistic, simplifying to the point of banality. Here, in this little nutshell is the whole tree? There is, however, some legitimacy in talking about a work rather than talking within a work; though I am not yet convinced it is the author's task to do the job that critics should.

There is more to asking than its mere service to knowledge. On its deeper levels, asking is itself both a species of reasoning and a resource for truth. If anything can be said in advance about this inquiry, it is precisely this: there is autonomous worth in asking. This realization determines the entire enterprise. It even affects the method or approach: I do not begin by considering the safely anchored ships in the harbor of knowledge, and then go backward, asking how we got there. Such an approach, taking established knowledge as the launching point, is doomed to unsuccess; for asking is always somehow in the middle, between knowing and ignorance. As Greek dramatists do, I begin already in that middle; realizing that it is this middle where reality lies; and total knowledge as well as blank ignorance are at best helpful abstractions. We begin in the middle because we are in the middle; we are askers far more profoundly than we are knowers or skeptics. Knowledge and ignorance, however, do not, when combined, somehow, tell us about asking; it is the other way around: only as askers can we make sense of knowledge or ignorance. It would therefore be extremely foolish to initiate an inquiry into what it means to ask by starting at either end. Airports do not account for flying; flying accounts for airports.

As early as the second chapter, the ontology and modality of being suspended in the middle is directly confronted, and the discovery learned from this is paramount. We not only exist, we are also aware of our being able to exist; our actuality reveals our enabling possibility. Self-reflectively conscious of this possibility entailed in our actuality, we find ourselves, distanced by the mirroring, suspended between necessity and nothingness; and this suspension is the foundation for our asking. We not only know this as a result of modal logic, we are also enabled by it to learn what it means to be thus suspended. This discovery of our being already suspended is the only meaningful point of departure that launches all that follows. It is, however, not a launch pad which, once used to get things started, is then disregarded or thrown away. Indeed, what this discovery of suspension itself means is learned only from what follows after it. There is, in this inquiry, considerable reiteration; the same point is repeated on deeper levels, for that is how we learn all truly important matters, from trusting and loving to appreciating art and learning to think deeply. Nevertheless, the modality and ontology of an enabling possibility remain so crucial to our understanding of what it means to ask, that it must initiate this curious task of asking about asking.

I am not unaware of the irony here. In seeking to show that asking is more fundamental than any specific answer, can I then provide a vast, schematic answer to the question? If so, then have I not shown it really is the answer that matters? Only a pedant would see this as a self-refutation; but honesty and a sense of completeness do require that irony itself deserve some critical analysis and even reiteration; these can be found in chapter 9 and chapter 11. I do not offer these reflections as a vast answering scheme or system. The apparent inconsistency or even paradox here is due to a rather naive view of what a question is; or indeed even what an answer is. It is part of the effort to show that, being in the middle, asking is not prohibited from discovering truth, and good answering never cuts itself off from its asking parentage.

Furthermore, as I discuss in the text, it is not a specific question or series of questions that can be fundamental, but asking as a phenomenon. To isolate a single question, and take it as if it were a linguistic unit, capable of analysis, is entirely retrograde to the whole spirit of this work. Various questions can, of course, be asked; and at times the asking that proceeds from the specific question as well as the asking that presupposes it, can reach fundamental levels; though not even the greatest of questions guarantees this will be done. In chapter 10 I consider seven astonishing and impressive questions which, when deeply probed, reveal remarkable discoveries. Even in these cases, however, it is not the questions themselves, but the asking that the questions promote, that achieves fundamentality. And it is this fundamentality that matters.

Although I am interested in accounting for how any questioning or asking occurs, my major concern is with what I call fundamental asking. In chapter 5 I analyze how ordinary questions are possible, and contrast them with fundamental asking. For this reason I begin, not with questioning as such, but with those bold and awesome confrontations that seem to demand the loftiest thought and the deepest probing. It must be done this way: we must ask greatly first; for the great explains the lesser; the small does not account for the large. Granted I must crawl before I walk, and walk before I dance; but it is only the great dancer who reveals what it means to move; it is only the study of the great commander that reveals what is accomplished by the thousands of foot soldiers.

In the prelude to what we call the First World War, the German Kaiser built a magnificent navy, perhaps not quite equal to the British, but formidable enough to cause the island kingdom to tremble; that navy was one of the central reasons why the war itself actually broke out. Yet, this powerful armada was ironically a prisoner of its own power; for Germany was reluctant to put such a massive weapon at risk. Here was a nice problem. Why have a great weapon if its loss is too great to risk? Is that not what mighty war machines are for? Not to cower safely in harbors ill designed for their success, but to venture out on the high seas where their awesome powers can be fully realized? It is difficult for me not to see a vague comparison with the Kaiser's armada and the present state of much of contemporary philosophy. Why have all that wonderful skill—genius even—all that sharp analytic reasoning, all these mental gifts and powers, and use them merely to assure us we really do know what is certain? The safe harbor here is knowledge; or rather the hegemony of epistemology that for the past hundred and fifty years or so has, like a defense-obsessed, cautionary strategy, kept us locked up in safe harbors, unable to venture out where the conflict is meaningful. This is not to denigrate all of the ongoing inquiry; it is merely to note the danger in too much caution, and to explain, in part, why the truth in and about asking cannot be found in the analysis of ordinary questions about bits of ordinary knowledge, much less the scarce items of certain knowledge. Yet, if knowledge cannot be the starting point, if we must begin in the middle, where is the middle? If we unleash the armada from the overly safe harbors, where do we send the fleet? Destroyers and patrol boats were part of those early navies, and their job was to search; now we use carrier-based AWACS. The inquiry, in other words, must include asking where to begin; there is no prior manual telling us where to go. To press the analogy a bit: we need not worry too much about this. So threatening was the Kaiser's fleet that its mere presence on the ocean's waterways would already attract the British; somewhere we will find our Jutland simply by sailing. It was a mighty fleet and ours is a mighty asking. It is not arrogance but reverence that says so.

1

Asking

We do not ask in order to learn, but learn in order to ask. Only those made wise through reading, reflection, celebrating, suffering, and courage can ask in this way, and when such asking takes place there is fundamental awe; for nothing—not the founding of empires nor the splitting of atoms nor the procreation of the species—is as spectacular as this. To ask greatly surpasses discovering greatly. The innumerable discover; only the rare and few ask. The loftiest arts ask and do not tell, the noblest sacrifice asks and tells not, the deepest thinkers do not tell; the deepest thinkers ask.

Quite rightly we mark the great as raising, not answering, questions. What they raise, however, are not ordinary questions but hitherto unrevealed askings which themselves reveal, as dawns reveal the daybreak still lurking darkly under eastern horizons, promising the new as an offering. In this manner the psalmist asks:

> When I consider thy heavens, the work
> of thy fingers, the moon and the stars,
> which thou hast ordained; What is
> man, that thou art mindful of him?

David first considered the stars and moon before he could ask the trembling, denuding, terrifying question. René Descartes asks: What kinds of things are there? To which a deeper Kant more deeply asks: How is it possible for me to think about the things that are? The worthier question stuns because, only as a question, does its truth emerge. Who taught Kant to ask like that?

The poet Auden asks: "O what authority gives existence its surprise?" We are surprised to hear this. Were we even aware that existence surprises? If art surprises it does so by revealing a hitherto latent question. David, too, was surprised. He did not ask merely what man is, but more profoundly, why God should even care about him. There does not seem, at first, to be much about us that should warrant such care. Perhaps David's asking shows us why. We matter because we ask.

Not all asking is of such lofty rank. We ask a hundred times a day, sometimes; and by this we are not surprised nor uplifted nor even made the slightest wiser even when the answers are forthcoming. Yet, in these ordinary, unspectacular questions there yet lurks something remarkable; though unnoticed, it quickly loses its surprising revelation and becomes entirely unremarkable. How do we ask at all? What does it mean to ask? Lest we trivialize our asking, we may perhaps want to qualify or insist: we seek the origin and meaning of fundamental asking—not mere buzzing curiosity or even a listing of the so-called great questions, already digested and packaged for us, as easy to swallow as pills. If we accept the cellophaned packet listing the established questions, together with several answers lest we be unfair, we may learn something but we truly ask nothing.

Fundamental asking is not entirely devoid of response. No question is meaningful without some sense of how it might be answered; or rather, we cannot ask without first knowing what we ask about, and this just means I am not radically ignorant when I ask. Plato shows us this in the *Meno*. Questions and answers obviously belong together, but it is the asking that matters more. This may amuse: asking about asking may be like packaging packages, putting smaller boxes into bigger ones; there is no reason to stop. Thinkers contemptuously label this an endless regress. After all, asking about how asking is possible is itself asking, so we find ourselves on a philosopher's treadmill or in a house of mirrors where reflections are themselves endlessly reflected. Such houses, though, are designed to confuse, and thereby amuse.

David considers first the heavens, the moon, and the stars; and only then asks: What is man? There is nothing in the moon or the stars that provides questioning about man. Thousands look at the firmament and ask nothing at all. Others look and ask lesser questions. What does David see in the moon and stars that makes him ask about his own place in the universe? He is not merely curious about the origin or makeup of the moon. Perhaps his asking is merely poetic fancy or a romantic sensitivity. Psalms are not science, nor are they philosophical treatises. The psalmist's question provokes all the same. If the moon and stars do not, of themselves, suffice to explain the question, then we must wonder seriously and not merely as a game. How does David raise the questions he asks? Is there a special, Kant-like category that accounts for it? Or does it take genius to leap from stars to man? Perhaps only David could ask like this. The first sentence of Aristotle's *Metaphysics* states that all men by nature desire to know. Does this explain David's psaltery? Is curiosity and not genius enough?

The desire to know cannot explain David's leap from stars to man. For this would turn the psalmist into an astronomer. Why does David, after looking at the stars and moon, not ask astronomers' questions? Some look and ask what caused the stars, or what the stars are made of. These are good questions, too. What gives David's question priority? If there is something about his questioning that is nobler—and it seems churlish to deny it—then it is manifest that not all asking is equal, that there are greater and lesser questions; and if not all asking is even, then we can fail at asking. How then do we succeed and fail at asking? If I ask how heavy the color green is or how tall justice is I am asking nonsense, whether I realize it or not. There are then, irrational questions. How can we be sure that David's question is not irrational?

A tocsin must be sounded against the plague, flippancy. Curiosity, the itch to know, idle fancy, stupid anthropomorphism, superstition, habit, the search for power—all these are sometimes promoted as the ground for asking metaphysical questions. But why should we accept answers which belittle the greatness of the question? The flippant may protest there are no great questions, and that to insist there are is merely a species of begging them. We are thus forced to ask: Are there great questions? But since this itself must be a great question, perhaps formally the greatest, the asking by itself seems to answer. What, we ask, is the greatest question of all? Answer: in the strictest, formal sense it must be the one just asked, for it seeks the fulcrum to lever the whole universe of questioning, and rank them. Even so, asking what the greatest question is in itself is not truly the greatest question. Perhaps David should have added to his psalm: "And why hast thou planted in us this power to ask?" The addendum is not necessary, of course, since the reader of the psalm is stunned by it already.

The same reader may also be moved to gratitude. The psalm tells us something about the psalmist, too. He becomes precious to us his inheritors, both trustful and doubtful, for his is a splendid nature, a beautiful sinner who seems to have a fawning, maddened, overly forgiving suitor, God, loving this radiant singer, boy, shepherd, king. We cannot blame God for becoming love-sotted, since we too are charmed deeply by him, though we know his faults, his passions, his indecent lusts, his secret, naked, time-warped visits to Michelangelo's studio and his irrepressible joy. Perhaps it is his joy that whelms us almost as much as his beauty; for it is joy that makes him sing the psalms, and the psalms reveal the asking we could not ask. It is possible that only the joyous can ask like that—we must explore this, too. Gratitude is a noble or at least ennobling passion, and if, through it, we learn to ask great secrets that otherwise remain unraised, then it would indeed be a fault of no little threat to our learning to be ungrateful.

The more we reflect on it, the more we are vexed. How did David move from his considering the moon and stars to ask such a naked question? How do we move from the contemplation of the world we know to questions that transcend our knowing? At the very least we should learn by these brief reflections on the Hebrew king that the method of inquiry cannot be initiated by posing ordinary questions as models to understand what asking means. "How's it going?" is a syntactically flawed, vulgar question, the dissection of which yields very little; but it is still a question, and hence deserves our inquiry. But it cannot be the questioned question. There is a common methodological fallacy of raising the trivial to get at the profound, to seek maximum wealth in minimalist penury. But if the discarded penny cannot open the treasure, and as seekers we are mendicants, where can we beg? The plutocrat's palace is guarded and gated, and the indigent unwelcome. As beggars though, we must learn how to ask.

If David's psalm tells us in part about David himself, we have the first clue to our own asking about asking. The asking reveals something about ourselves. What does it reveal? That we are finite. Asking exposes our naked vulnerability as finite. Just as nakedness has both a positive and a negative sense, so does our finitude. We are not all-wise, but neither are we all-ignorant. A little game of modal logic can be played: We exist; hence our nonexistence is not necessary; but we can die, so neither is our existence necessary. We are suspended then between impossibility and necessity. The obviousness of this modal inference cannot entirely eclipse its radiance. Where do we get such magnificent concepts as necessity, contingency, possibility, and impossibility? These are big notions. Even to think them seems to make us very clever, very powerful indeed. They are, we are assured by the logicians, inherent in the very business of thought. We don't learn these things by running into them as items in the environment. To be finite, then, does not, apparently, prohibit us from confronting the infinite. Perhaps asking is possible just because the finite abuts the infinite.

What do these intimidating logical terms have to do with the earlier terms about David, such as joy, wonder, gratitude, and beauty? We are the same ones who ask each set of questions, even though the flavor of the asking seems changed. If the first topic about asking seems to emerge as our finitude, surely the second must be our language. For David's psalm is a wonder of language, and at least in the English translation of Shakespeare's day, 1611 to be exact, it is sheer poetry. There seems to be some magical core in the very essence of language that allows us to ask. The poetry inherent in the psalm may well be what accounts for the raising of its great question. Simple, speechless animals seem to exhibit curiosity in their behavior, but they cannot, lacking real language, raise these self-reflective questions. It is self-reflective language that allows us to distinguish both the necessary from the possible, as well as gratitude from dependence. We are not merely finite, but self-reflectively finite; and it is this that makes us intimate with notions like necessity and infinity. The necessary is not the mere abstract negation of our own contingency; it is rather the concrete confrontation with our self-reflective contingency, which oddly *as* self-reflective is not merely contingent any more: we are necessarily contingent—a comic discovery which may make us laugh a bit, the way joy does.

Even ordinary questions show this. "Where am I?" does not ask about the spot I now locate, but about the broader atlas that relates various interconnected spots. "Show me where I am on the map." The larger map alone makes sense of the question. Without the possibility of the map, the question would always be meaningless. It is this questioning that makes mapmakers do their work. David's question demands some sense of the vast panorama of possible entities other than ourselves—which may in part explain why his contemplation of the heavens and stars provokes his question. "What is a cheetah?" provokes: "the swiftest of the large, carnivorous cats"; we leap from the individual to the species, the species to the genus, suggesting that questioning is the primeval reaching beyond the given and the immediate. Even if these dry and formal considerations are correct, the question about such questioning is staggering. What is it about us that accounts for reaching beyond ourselves like that? Does asking account for transcendence?

There is a great danger here. We cannot reach some extra-worldly platform from which we gain an encompassing vision; for where would that platform be? To say it is outside the world cheats on what the word *world* means; but to say it is in the world seems to deny it can provide the externalist vision. We must always ask from within the world, even and especially when we ask about the world. It is as lovers that we ask about love and as knowers that we ask about knowledge and as sufferers that we ask about suffering; so likewise it is as dwellers in the world—and only as world-dwellers—that we ask about the world. These discoveries suggest that if asking does provide some transcendence beyond what is given, it also insists that this transcendence is yet rooted in what we already are. It is only as askers that we ask about asking.

There is another point. We do not always ask *about;* we can also ask *for;* and this discovery needs some reflection. Strictly, we ask for what is bestowed, not for what is a right. I should not have to ask for justice; I should demand it. That I sometimes do ask for what is due me by right may simply reveal a certain modality of civility: "May I please have my card back?" may sound more polite than demanding; but if it is truly my card I have a right to it, and asking for it suggests otherwise. In social contexts though, civility must count above all else. There is room for caution, however; we do not want to lose an important truth. I can only ask for a boon; it need not be given. To ask a favor implies the request may legitimately be denied; and if the favor be granted, it must be seen not as an earned wage but as a bestowal. Merely because we consider the heavens does not give us the right to demand we know about who we are. This kind of asking asks for a gift; perhaps the very asking itself is a bestowal—a bestowal that bestows.

Yet, not altogether so. Were I to learn by dint of experience and reflection that without sunlight and water the plant dies, it seems there is an authority built into that very learning that permits me, de jure, as it were, to ask whether sunlight alone or water alone or only both together are causes of the plant's success. To ask which are the causes thus seems a right inherent in my knowing, and not a boon. To ask the psalmist's question asks for a boon and not a right. How do we understand this difference? Is the difference itself merely apparent, or is it real? Do we ask the psalmist's question but demand the botanist's answer? Perhaps asking for boons is entirely unequal to asking questions. David may ask for enlightenment from God; but Kant, clanging away at the machinery of universal consciousness, finds the exact same question, *Was ist der Mensch?* and ranks it as the ultimate. Is the psalmist bestowed while the philosopher earns? Is it the same question if earned or bestowed?

Mention of the word *authority* raises yet another question. Is reasoning—that is, thinking with authority—inherent in asking? Is asking essential for reasoning? Perhaps our definition ought to be that we are the asking animal, and only because of this essence as asking can we really think at all. Certainly if asking is that modality of our consciousness that allows us to grasp, however vaguely, the broader spectra, then it would indeed be central, and not peripheral, to reasoning. Some thinkers recognize the centrality of asking, and accordingly identify true thought as dialectical. The essence of dialectic is that the achievement of one kind of knowledge necessarily opens a new kind of question, which in turn returns to discover the original question that has now been transformed, and so we must ask again, though on a loftier level.

It is not merely dialectical thinkers, however, that recognize the authority inherent in asking. There is, indeed, a great peril in reifying the dialectical stages, as if the relation between questioning and answering somehow constitutes the metaphysical structure of the universe. Dialectical theorists often succumb to this toxic enmity, for once such progression is systemized, the paradox is that no more questions are possible—which poisons dialectic to death. Nevertheless, in spite of the peril, there is an attraction to fusing, if not reducing, the method with the doctrine. Whatever truth is, surely it must be the parent and not the offspring of questions. Truth and reasoning cannot, for those of us who consider the stars and then ask about man, be entirely separated.

Asking seems then to reveal the truth about our finitude, about our language, about our reasoning, and ultimately about the meaning of truth itself. How easily we fall into the trap and ask wrongly: What is the correct theory of truth? We must insist on our asking: what is the truth about truth? Whatever truth may be, it cannot be revealed in a theory. Theorophiles abound; they are the pickpockets of academia, slick-fingered petty thieves who thrive in noisy crowds, whose ubiquity cheapens a festival into a tourist trap. They and their fellow-felons, the labelers, are the defilers of the holy precinct of truth precisely because theories and labels purloin the sacrament: they answer stolen questions first, and then fit the question to the asking. The ritual they defile by this inversion is philosophy itself.

Finitude, language, reasoning, and truth—all these both follow and are presupposed if asking about asking is to take place seriously. But reflections on reflection, on boons and rights, on joy and vexations, are also needed. The cursory reconnaissance of what lies before us may intimidate the asker at the onset. Courage too, then, is required; which is why this asking is infrequent.

We ask ultimate questions even though we ourselves fall far short of ultimacy. We ask about death and God, love and suffering, beauty and justice, good and evil, knowing full well such questioning alters us fundamentally, so that, altered, we are transformed beyond our innocence. Like Eve, the simple act of asking about good and evil renders us unfit for Eden's tranquility. Even so, it is not clear that we would unask such transforming questions even if we could; for though the loss of innocence may disturb, the loss of responsible reflection is even dearer. However greatly we ask, the greater peril always lurks that in responding we forget what the asking has done to us. The terrified lover may ask whether he ought to ask whether his love is returned. In asking about asking he reveals the dreadful truth about loving. Is it worse to learn she might not requite, or to remain in anguish about not learning? How can so much joy depend on someone else's decision? How can so much joy depend on so much suffering? Were it better not to love at all than to suffer so in love's purgatory? The question about whether he should ask may well be far more devastating than the question whether she, too, loves. Of such comic, though no less serious, anguish are great torments and greater artworks born. The surprise may even be—relief in her denial. How soon the wounded earth forgets the plow. Of this asking, though, nothing should be forgotten.

2

Possibility

After asking, or perhaps as a part of it, the psalm continues: man has been made "a little lower than the angels," yet is "to have dominion over the works of thy hands." We certainly seem to be suspended between whatever is highest and whatever is lowest, however we may understand this. Suspension seems to be of our essence, whether we express it in terms of the psalmist's theology or otherwise: we neither know everything nor do we lack knowledge entirely; our existence is neither necessary nor impossible. It is as possible that we hang suspended between everything and nothing, God and beast, the absolute and the nugatory. To ask is to make possible the possible, for when I ask beyond my knowledge, I project from that knowledge to the possibility of it in terms of the greater scheme that locates it. "When is she coming?" projects the clock or the calendar, and beyond them to the general reckoning of sequential time; "Why must we suffer?" projects—and hence makes possible—the assumed synthesis of purpose, or perhaps meaning.

In moments of genius this projection or making-possible seems among the highest of our accomplishments. When Mendeleyev saw that certain elements had different atomic weights, he projected beyond that observation to the possibility of a table based solely on progressive numbering, launching a fervid period of looking for as-yet-undiscovered elements that we now knew must be there. The stunning speed with which the empty slots were provided with named discoveries attests to the brilliance of his new questioning: not, *what* elements do we know, but *where* do they, as well as the as-yet-undiscovered, *belong?* When Darwin began collecting the vast variety of new species, he learned to stop asking for purposes, raising a simple, historical question that eventually led to actual but hitherto unobserved phenomena, mutations, changing a science forever. We note these highlights of our history, and rightly note the essential role of hypotheses in science. Hypotheses, however, are not projected answers but retro-seeking questions. It is an error, then, simplemindedly to account for these great scientific discoveries by believing that *first* we hypothesize, and *then* seek empirical evidence either to support or refute. For the great hypotheses were great questions that arose out of deep immersion in, and deep vexation with, the phenomena that begged for an asking of a possibility that both transcends as it unifies, and belongs as it surpasses. Anyone can imagine systems, and most of these projections are silly and pompous. When Bach, however, as master musician, saw the need to ask for a new graphic representation of the musical possibilities, he enriched both the reading and writing of music. When Aeschylus recognized the possibility of the third player, he asked the further possibility of unlimited *dramatis personae;* and modern drama, based on the interaction of developing characters, was born. Both Bach and Aeschylus, however, were first already accomplished artists, musician or poet; their projections did not begin, but arose out of, their arts. Only a reverential monotheist could ask as David does. Neither polytheist nor deist—and certainly not atheist—could ask what the psalmist asks.

We ask about our suspension between the highest and the lowest, and suggest that this suspension is creative projection, i.e., making-possible. We note, however, that this reflection is itself troubling. Sketches from genius perhaps help to keep the inquiry from hyperabstraction, but we cannot be satisfied with anecdotal insight. The issue is to take our understanding of possibility away from the sheer formality of the modal logician and concretize it existentially as the phenomenon of asking. To do this undermines the merely spatial metaphor of "suspension," a metaphor that suggests a passive, almost inert, state, as a bridge suspends between two banks of the river. But the term *suspension* has another, dramatic meaning, as when Sophocles builds almost unendurable suspense in his plays. Here *suspense* means the concrete confrontation of possibility as it either threatens or promises; it is, if you will, how we "feel" our own being possible. In our witness of the drama, we do not merely consider possible abstractions, as we might do in assessing possible moves on a chess board; rather we directly experience the anxiety of being able to discover what, in the "actual" past, may doom us to an inevitable perdition—though this is endured without the need of trying to avoid it, given the aesthetic distance of the stage.

What gives the dramatic revelation of possibility its singular concreteness is that the suspense builds between what comes before and what comes after, though inverted from the usual logic. The critic identifies this correctly as beginning *in medias res*. To begin after the beginning—in the "middle"— may seem almost comically contradictory, but this aesthetic device deserves our reflection. What we wish to do here is realize that we seek suspenseful possibility within the actual, not the mere abstract possibility of the nonactual. All that is actual must also be possible, but not all that is possible need be actual, so it might seem that the best access to possibility would be its nonactual modality. The study of Greek drama may help to show that the putative superiority of the nonactual over the actual as the basis for learning possibility is really a distraction. It is far more difficult, but far more exciting, to raise the meaning of possibility as it lurks in the actual. What does it mean to say that, what is also can be?

The play begins with Oedipus already in a dire dilemma brought about by his past actions in the context of his past origins. The future looms as feral cruelty, but only if the king continues his search for the truth. We the audience learn his past as well as his destiny at the same pace, as the story unfolds. Jocasta urges him to quit his dreadful inquiry, for she senses it were better not to know. As we learn of his youthful ventures, the possibility— the asking—takes on a curious inevitability. In this way the present unfolding of his past as our futural learning as audience seems to make the decisive past the tyrant over the unchangeable future, which of course is backwards from our ordinary understanding in which the past is locked away and unchangeable and only the future is open to our will. Oedipus's future thereby seems in the thrall of what is uncovered as past. The suspense, which rivets us, is therefore less dependent on what will happen, and turns rather to what has happened. Granted that this is the structure of success for the tragic play, what does it mean? The actual (the past, what really did happen) becomes the possible—i.e., the source of suspense, whereas the future becomes the inevitable, as dramatically fated. Along with Jocasta we almost want to stop our ears to keep from hearing about the past that dooms the truth-seeking king.

This suspense is by no means dependent on ignorance. The audience already knows the plot; indeed the more thoroughly we master the artwork, the deeper our rapture in its suspense. But how, we ask, is it possible to be in suspense when we already know what will happen? What else is suspense except uncertainty as to the future? But in this remarkable milieu, the drama, it is the certainty of what must happen that provides greater, almost unendurable, suspense. Why? Partly because the mere uncertainty of what will happen is a distraction from the deeper questioning: What does it *mean* to discover the bleak future as already determined by a nonbleak, "free" past? The past becomes the arena of the possible, even though, as past, it must be actual. The audience is in suspense as the actual past is disclosed in terms of its ability to be—its possibility. This suspense is primordial or fundamental asking. It does not ask what happens, since we already know that (and such knowledge can be achieved by the simple reading of a plot summary) but rather asks what it means to lock up our future as a prisoner of our past—a discovery which can only be achieved by the actual witness on stage of the hero learning, in waxing terror, the meaning of his own past.

The simple modal logic therefore opens a purse of wondrous affluence. We say innocently enough: all that is actual is also possible, and think no more about it because, like all purely logical truths, it seems too obvious. Yet, to think the actual *as* being in part its possibility, invests at a lofty rate of interest, compounding at the highest advantage to the investor. For it is possibility deposited in the actual that opens the exchequer of asking. The mere actuality of something does not finance the raising of fundamental questioning nor does the merely formal possibility in logic; only the possibility within the actual can do this. The sample from Attic tragedy gives us our first taste by inverting the normal logic of actual events. I cannot undo the past but I can, in part at least, affect the future; Sophocles turns this around, so that Oedipus cannot alter his future and we the audience are gripped with the suspense of watching the *past* unfold. It is therefore not only our freedom (to act), but also our fate (to be) that is vitalized by possibility, and hence asking.

Possibility is far more than the mere recognition of options. We discover the logician's modalities by our capacity to imagine. Students are asked to consider whether the color of the wall is contingent or necessary. Need the wall be painted green? No, I can imagine it painted blue. The contingency of the wall's color is recognized by the student's power to imagine it otherwise. The imagination then becomes central to our ability to make distinctions within modal logic. The faculty functions as its name suggests: it is an image-making power. Some images apparently come to us solely from our empirical observations, but others we make up. The ability to "make up" images is imagination, and apparently this imagination lies at the very basis of learning modal logic—at least to the extent to which we can distinguish the necessary from the contingent, making us aware of the difference between what must be from what may be. We may even add the adjective *creative* to the noun *imagination* giving the faculty a certain originality. But this seems almost as backward as what Sophocles does on the stage. To speak of creative imagination seems to suggest the entirely free, something unfettered by chains of the already established, grounded only in the spontaneity of our seminal originality—yet now we suggest that the very rigorous statutes of modal logic itself are grounded in the creative imagination. For I ask myself: Can I creatively imagine the wall being a color other than it is now? to which I say "yes"; and then ask: Can I creatively imagine the wall not taking up space, to which I say "no," I must see the wall as spatial. The so-called creative imagination thus produces an entirely uncreative rule that governs all thought that limits even the imagination. The new question now stuns: How did I go from a freely creative act to the discovery of grim, necessary, inevitable laws that make up the most authoritarian of all realizations: modal logic itself? Does the origin of this logic in the creative imagination mean I can change at my whim the rules of logic? Curiously, no. Does the inevitability of these iron laws mean the origin of them is not really in the creative imagination? No. Then how do we go from the creative to the necessary? How does the actual lead to the possible (or the stars lead David to ask about man)?

The mere application of the discovered rules of logic cannot answer this question, but neither can the mere appeal to the faculty of the imagination. To ask whether we can imagine the wall another color enables. To enable means more than the mere discovery of what is the case, it is an active, establishing, granting event. To teach a student to use the violin enables him to make music; to teach him how to reflect on the limits of his imagination enables him to do modal logic. To show him a performance of *Oedipus Tyrannos* enables him to celebrate his finitude. The crutch enables the one-legged to walk. To enable thus *makes* possible; it does not merely discover what *is* possible. Asking itself is an enablement. Consider a banal, everyday, unremarkable claim: the lamp is on the table. The eager jackals of analysis immediately leap upon this as a carcass, tearing and chewing and devouring it into its smallest parts, seeking to find in this so-called proposition all the things they deem worth knowing. Yet, who would make such a claim? Why would anyone say it? It is, if you will, taken by itself, an almost unimaginable event: someone saying out of the blue, devoid of any and all context, "The lamp is on the table." Why say it? Indeed we *can* imagine a situation in which we might say it, as we might respond to a question asking where the lamp is. Without this question, however, the sentence truly is meaningless, for it is not anything anyone would say noncontextually. The question enables the answer. It makes it possible by making it intelligible. In this way, the possible—seen here as the prior question—is found in the actual: the claim itself. It is the asking that enables the response. This point is not unique to this inquiry. Collingwood, for entirely different reasons and with an entirely different agenda, also points out the priority of the question.

The suggestion that the laws of logic depend on the power of the logician to imagine, and thus to discover what cannot be imagined, raises two disturbing, interrelated questions. First, is all fundamental asking about the asker? Second, is all fundamental asking always provoked by the realization of a limit to possibility, requiring a transcendental stepping back? The answer to both is yes; but even here the answer is vacuous without digging more deeply into what is entailed in the asking. The guiding theme of this suggestion remains that the fundamental grasp of possibility lies in the possibility-within-the-actual rather than the possibility inherent in what is contrary to fact. To emphasize this we can consider an actual, historical phenomenon that revealed a great, hitherto unexpected truth, by focusing upon the challenge to what is possible in the minds of the participants, rather than to the present-day, enlightened "answer."

In 1521, the thirty-one sailors who had survived after they circumnavigated the globe under Magellan's leadership arrived back in Europe. Their tales excited great interest and their exploits received due praise, but their log seemed in error—it was a day off. We read in our modern, casual, almost bemused, accounts that they had unknowingly crossed the international dateline. There are two things that are wrong here. They did not cross the dateline, since it did not then exist as a convention. (It could have been drawn anywhere, but convenience suggested the central Pacific.) The second error is our amusement at their difficulty in comprehending what happened. Consider what these intrepid men were asked to conceive as possible. I can, at a certain spot, sit down to lunch on Tuesday at noon, look across at my neighbor and see him sitting down to lunch on Wednesday at noon. That, the sturdy Portuguese sailor would say, is monumentally silly. It cannot be both Tuesday and Wednesday at the same time, especially at almost the same spot. Were we to go far enough north, or south, where longitudes get closer together, we can walk back and forth from yesterday to tomorrow at will and at ease. This is nonsense; something is deeply wrong here. Most great discoveries were not this unexpected. We knew someone would fly eventually, and the Wright brothers simply did it first. Even the ancient Greeks thought flying, as well as going to the moon, were possible, but they would have blanched at walking into yesterday. The fiction of the international dateline unfortunately misleads the contemporary student, distracting him from a prodigy of creative thinking, that does not need the dateline at all.

We must think two things. We live on a spinning orb that completes its cycle in what we call a day. Any point, such as a town, on that orb goes through the cycle in what we divide by ancient Egyptian convention into twenty-four hours. (Too bad it wasn't thirty-six, for then the time zones would have agreed with the longitudes.) Any given spot therefore circles the orb; but it is also possible for us, as travelers, to circle the orb. Our circling it as travelers, conjoined with our point of departure to which we eventually return also circling it, means that we have gone around *twice*, once at the speed of twenty-four hours, the other at speeds less than that, depending on the conveyance. Once we realize that the new question asks what it means to live on a spinning orb *and* to be able to travel around it, our entire notion of time is altered. Not only is the dateline, unlike the equator, for example, a mere convention, so is the division of the day into twenty-four hours. These conventions are projections of *abstract* possibilities that provide convenience, not true understanding. The circling itself is not a convention, nor is the beguilement that faces anyone who crosses the dateline; even today it gives many travelers a funny feeling, as if the world is playing tricks.

The Portuguese sailors of the sixteenth century, however, who did not have a dateline, found limits to their imagination that were both false and true. They thought it impossible to walk back and forth between days; and of course in one sense they are right and we are "wrong." If by the term *day* we mean the passage of twenty-four hours, we simply cannot go back to yesterday. Only if the word *day* becomes the assigned convention of certain specific labels, such as Thursday and Friday, can I walk into "yesterday." It is we, who play with conventions as if they were real, that are confused. The Portuguese sailors were wrong only insofar as they did not see the need to account for being able to circle the orb *twice*, and hence the need to establish what is a counter-intuitive convention. (They, of course, went the wrong way to circle twice; they "lost" a day by circling against the way the world turns.) There are subtleties here. If by *day* we mean sunrise to sunrise, the

Portuguese did not notice that as they traveled westward there was a little more than twenty-four hours on some days. These increments were simply too small to notice, given the crudeness of their chronometers; but by the time they returned these minuscule increments added up to twenty-four hours. This, then, is the most important point for our inquiry: one does not need a dateline to tell this story.

The puzzlement of the navigators was very real. It took a fairly long time to figure it out, even though all the necessary facts were long ago readily known. We already knew in the sixteenth century that we lived on a spinning orb and that we could circumnavigate it. We had to think what it meant; and the vexation with logs that seemed a day out of whack with the calendar required a new kind of asking, a new kind of possibility.

This possibility, however, was not an abstract, nonactuality; the new possibility lurked already in the fact of Portuguese sailors having circumnavigated the globe and the apparent fact of having "lost" a day. They had not really lost it, of course; they had been taking little bites out of it every time their day from sunrise to sunrise took a little longer than twenty-four hours, due to their chasing the setting sun. By the time they got back they had eaten a whole day without realizing it. The possibility of this was in the actuality of what they had done and the bewilderment of having seemed to have lost a day. This means, however, that it is the actual, befuddled navigator on whom the new possibility falls as a demand for clarification; or rather, the possibility itself becomes the explanation of the already actual.

The dateline is an abstraction; it is a made-up possibility. But the possibility within the actual navigators seeking to make sense of what they did, is actual, though what makes it worthy of our thinking is the actual as, or in terms of, possibility. Thus, we do not need to rely solely on artworks such as *Oedipus Tyrannos* to realize this importance: the actual is *interestingly* possible.

In this sea of reflections it may be needful now to do a "dead reckoning" to find where we are. The suggestion was made that fundamental questions require a projection of possibility. A hint from the continuation of David's psalm suggested that we are somehow "suspended" between extremes. Although David suspends us between angels and beasts, we restated this suspension between necessity and impossibility; between these two are usually found the actual and the possible. Since all that is actual is also possible, we decided to focus on that as the basis of our suspension. To make suspension active, being in suspense, we reflected on Sophocles' great tragedy and found a curious inversion of our normal understanding of possibility and actuality. This however, may seem a purely aesthetic device—though subsequently we found it elsewhere as well. Possibility in both its actual and contrary-to-fact conditionality was seen to lie in our ability to create images, the faculty of the imagination. This faculty was seen as the origin of modal logic, an origination that itself is something of a paradox. To escape from the putative limits of aesthetics, and the algorithmic formality of logic, we sought an example of how possibility reveals more in the actual than in the abstract, and reflected on the Portuguese sailors "losing" a day in circumnavigating the globe. In this way, the phrase "the possibility within the actual" is given a concrete manifestation. This is important in the attempt to grasp what possibility means in terms of fundamental asking. It is *not* the mere consideration of endless options, limited only by the outlawry of self-contradiction.

What, then, does it mean to be possible? If we bracket the purely formal notion of "not entailing a contradiction," we discover something fundamental about our being in the world as askers. This inevitably directs attention to ourselves; although the wall could possibly be green rather than blue, such possibility is not really in the wall but in our imagination. Only as self-reflective can we ask about our own possibility, and thus only as self-reflective can we discover what it means to ask. All fundamental asking is therefore always about the asker. We therefore revisit the earlier question, changing it from "What does it mean to say that what is, also can be?" to "What does it mean to say I am and I can be?"

We ask about our possibility-as-actual and not merely our actuality; and because this is fundamental asking, we are not even sure exactly what form it should take. Who am I? What is my origin? How do I fit into the grander scheme of things? Do I matter? All of these are worthy questions, perhaps, but none is sufficient. Perhaps in questioning each deeply enough, all the others eventually emerge. To ask how I, who am, also can be, is to focus on our realization that possibility somehow constitutes my essence. We may identify this quality as freedom, but there is great peril in doing so, freighted as the term *freedom* is with dubious metaphysics. Besides, to raise the question in this context now seems out of place. It may be that only as free can we ask about our meaning, but it is not obvious that turning the question entirely around may not be a truer asking. Nevertheless, the term seems to suggest itself in raising the question about possibility; but it deserves only a brief mention here to serve as a hint.

It is not merely that we are suspended between the highest and lowest, God and beast, but that we are reflectively conscious of such suspension, and this seems to be the basis of our making possible our actuality. To be able to be who and what we are requires awareness of our suspension. Upon reflection it becomes obvious that David's "considering" is not merely of the heavens but already of his own ability to consider; the move from the firmament to man is now less shocking. No matter how large or small our existence seems with regard to the universe, our asking about it discloses a range greater than galaxies since it is we who, in "considering" them, transcends them; and transcendence is the realm of the possible. This vast transcendence is possibility; not a mere abstract, but a concrete, possibility; it achieves a concretely possible unity, not a mere abstract unity (such as the dateline), for the asking itself is not abstract. Does this mean that our own being-possible is necessarily connected in some way with suspension? Are we, metaphysically, always and already *in medias res*—perhaps "smack-dab" in the middle?

Consider the speculative cosmology lurking behind the wilder imaginings of the parascientist. Starting with myself, apparently I can imagine, perhaps ad infinitum, each unit made of smaller units, the smallest of which is ultimately real. Or, if there is no final "smallest," the smaller the unit the closer to ultimate reality we become. From stone, to molecule, to atom, to quark, to the next smallest, we get ever closer to reality. But I can also imagine going the other way: from a person I become a speck on the globe, the globe a speck on the galaxy, the galaxy a speck on supergalactic units, these as specks on the universe. The real is the biggest. We feel humbled by all this; yet curiously arrogant and "enlightened" by making ourselves so far removed from what is basic reality. Yet, as we go vastly into the small that explains everything, or vastly into the vast that explains everything, at no time do we find instances of mind. We do not hear atomic reductionists believing that thirty steps below the quark there are decisions, speculations about the universe, guilt feelings, love, or even logic and science. Nor do we imagine supergalaxies thinking about yesterday or what it means to be a supergalaxy. Such accounts are deemed anthropomorphic. We should not ascribe human-like qualities, including thinking, to entities like quarks or galaxies. Is mind, then, only in the middle? In the exact middle, and nowhere else? Should we not even worry about anthropomorphizing ourselves?

If thinking occurs only in the middle, not among galaxies or quarks, then we have a problem, for it seems we are utterly medieval: once more we are the center of the universe. We may, perhaps, imagine other planets in other galaxies that have thinking beings on them, but if so they are middle sized—nowhere near as large as galaxies nor as wee as quarks. We may, of course, imagine that our galaxy is really a tiny brain cell of a vast, thinking giant—for speculation has no shame—but we do not think that this galactic giant's *thinking* in any way illuminates our universe, any more than *our* thinking makes up our own tiny brain cells. Such a giant is a purely speculative, meaningless abstraction that adds nothing to our understanding. Is this not medievalism gone amok? Are we, the middle-sized, the only thinkers? If it is anthropomorphism to believe quarks and galaxies *think*— and it would be superstitious silliness to believe it—then the middle-sized really is central, for only we, the middle-sized, think. We are aware of quarks and galaxies but they are not aware of us.

If, indeed, thinking requires that smaller units always must make up larger ones, and that whatever is, must be contained in some greater vessel, itself contained by an even greater, then thinking would have to be only in the middle, for it would have to be able to go both ways. But in neither direction, the greater nor the smaller, would we find other thinkers, so as thinkers we are truly suspended. Such a claim may be a species of sublime silliness—silly because all cosmological speculation is so abstract it makes no sense, sublime because it shows the silliness of such abstract speculation even as it reveals again the concrete centrality of mind. Thinking as a concrete reality destroys every conceivable cosmology, which is always entirely abstract, even when it seems materialistic. Thales' account of the world as water is abstract, not concrete. Thinking is the one reality that cannot be accounted for by nonthinking elements. Thinking reveals not only the possible, but also what cannot be, the impossible, and that is something *no* abstractly conceived, cosmological entity can do.

When we consider nonfactual possibilities, their number is unlimited, for anything (except self-contradictions) is possible in this sense. But when we consider the possible in terms of its enabling the actual, only one account is ultimately sound, though approaches to it may be varied. It is astonishing how many speculative accounts of the universe make sense of everything except the speculative thinker himself; but speculation is projective thinking par excellence, and hence absolutely depends on the creative projector or enabler. It may have seemed a facetious remark to suggest above that perhaps we should fear anthropomorphizing ourselves, but in fact this "fear" is precisely our contemporary superstition. If it be superstitious to infuse nonconscious beings with consciousness, it is likewise superstitious to deny consciousness (or "reduce" it to nonconscious description) to actually conscious beings, especially if that denial is based on the fear of appearing old-fashioned, and "hence" superstitious. Whatever the world ultimately is, it contains within it beings that can and do reflect on it; and whatever we are, we are already and always within the world, and not a mere formally understood subject "outside" it.

Enabling thinking just is the power of the self to include the self in our speculating of the possible. The inclusion of our selves into the world is speculating from actuality; it makes possible—enables—the actual. If this be so, however, purely formal considerations no longer suffice, for the formal by definition is not limited by the actual. For the thinker, however, neither is the actual limited to the actual; for it is the enabling of creative possibility that reveals what the actual means. Thus, purely formal (abstract) speculation and mere factual recognition of the environment do not exhaust the range of our thinking. There is a special kind of thinking that allows us to consider what enables (makes possible) the actual. This power is asking; or, to be more precise, this power to enable our own actuality, though not to cause it, is fundamental asking.

It may be noticed that in all the concrete reflections about possibility suggested in this chapter, the nature and essential meaning of our being the questioner emerges. From the speculative hypotheses of the great scientists, to Aeschylus and Bach, and even to the Portuguese navigators, the deepest thinking requires some sense of being a thinker; this in turn is seen as speculating about possibility (*not* options), which in turn is seen as the power to ask. It is of critical importance to realize that we do not ask the actual as possible but the possible as actual. That is, we do not consider, in an Aristotelian manner, the vast array of the possible (potentiality), and then recognize the few which somehow emerge as actual, as if actuality were a synthetic predicate added on to possibles; rather we ask for possibility within an actual. This can be done only *of* self-reflective, asking beings *by* self-reflective asking beings. When the Portuguese navigators returned with a day seemingly missing, the thinkers of the world were required, not to learn new things, but to consider what they already knew in the light of new and deeper reflection. Thus, they themselves, as thinkers, become the targets of their inquiry. They did not speculate abstractly to nonactual options, but simply reflected more deeply on what they already knew; for it is not obvious that a youngster even today, looking at a globe, would infer that days mean different things when traveling around the turning orb. He would have to think deeply about it, and about himself as one who asks. He would have to enable himself, and such enabling reveals him as questioner.

These samples, however, are all indirect. What happens when we raise the possibility of our own meaning directly? We shift from our being as questioner to our being as self-questioner. I exist; but what does it mean that I exist *and* that I ask about my existence? The conjunctive *and* reveals itself as essential, not only because what follows the *and* may be in part an answer to what precedes it—what it means for me to exist is to ask what it means to exist—but also because without the addendum the original question may be swallowed up by abstractive projections that themselves have no ground. It should be clear by now that however we question ourselves, the actual raising of the question comes from an already established attitude of reflective asking. We do not stumble across the question, What is man? as if it were a pure, context-free, ungrounded item on a list of given problems. It is David's joyous theism coupled with his speculative, poetic genius that allows him to raise it; it is Kant's hard labors of critique, coupled with his inheritance of the Enlightenment, that brings him to it; just as it is the fascination with conceptual games that lead many contemporary speculators away from it. We ask about our own being able to be, seeking this possibility only within our actuality. In no way does this imply a subjectivist relativism, any more than Bach's universal genius is available only to German Lutherans, even though it is precisely Bach's singular piety that informs his genius. The universal is always concretely grounded, else it would only and ever be abstract.

What does possibility mean if it is the concrete possibility within the actual? It is the ground of meaning that is exposed by the paradox of familiar unfamiliarity. To ground is to render thinkable, precisely when unthinking acceptance is most friendly, yet when its very friendliness becomes alien. To ground is to render thinkable: I cannot raise questions about what a day means until and unless the habit of living day by day is so ingrained as to be unthought, and unless some violence, such as losing a day in circling the globe, rips the unthought into needful asking.

We think. This phenomenon itself is familiar enough to lose sight of its origin. What provokes us to think? Asking? The familiar wrenched from its familiarity into a new kind of strangeness? But if we ourselves are the ground of thinking—that is, we make thinking about ourselves possible—then in making possible our actuality we make ourselves strange to ourselves. There is nothing either familiar or strange about idle speculation on abstract possibilities; but there is both strangeness and familiarity in grounding—making thinkable—our own being-possible. Thus, to think our actuality in terms of possibility removes us from reliance on our actuality to the precarious transcendence of making our own meaning possible. We transcend, not as those possessing knowledge, but as askers of our own asking. There is nothing arbitrary about this. We ask only because truth matters, and the only route to truth about ourselves is in asking about the possibility of being ourselves. This possibility is itself meaningful because it can be accepted or rejected. The acceptance or rejection of possibilities within the actual is not restricted to future options, but pervades the entire range of what is meaningful.

Suppose I am, at this moment, in a state of such rapturous joy that I can celebrate everything that makes it possible. Suppose also that, in reflecting on my past, I recall an event of dreadful, excruciating suffering which I desperately wish had never occurred, and which entails a horrifying realization of my own obscene guilt. This prior agony is an essential part of who I am; the pain, the guilt, the revulsion at my own weakness, the shame inherent in its reflection, and the shudder of cowardly fear that I should ever have to endure it again, all have influenced me and molded me to my present character. The joy I now feel is singularly mine, but as mine is made possible by who I am, a possibility that in part requires my past agony. I must wish that the past agony had never happened, but without it I would not be who I am now, and I cannot wish myself different from who I am now, since I alone, as what I am, make possible this radiant rapture of joyous ecstasy. Perhaps the scathing torment has made me vulnerable, and only as vulnerable in this singular way is the depth of my joy possible. There is a dilemma here of sorts. It would be insulting to dismiss this as an instance of learning from my mistakes, or as maturing through harsh experience. Do I affirm my shame to keep my joy? Do I restrain my joy by censuring my shame? Do I cheat by taking refuge in some divine plan? Or do I, in the unshamed embrace of this radiant triumph find that the very dilemma curiously sparks an added intensity to the ecstasy? These very questions themselves may exacerbate the joy by revealing the authority of reflection that accompanies it, as well as the happy confusion inherent in the asking. These are conflicts, not contradictions. Happy confusions are possible because I need not know the explanation to confront the meaningfulness within the confusion. Who are we, knowing of our faults, that thou art mindful of us? So may ask an unworthy lover who is unexpectedly requited, or a sinful psalmist who worships a seemingly forgiving God, or an intoxicated thinker high on the highest asking. Joy itself is curious enough, for in its highest instances there seems no adequate justification precisely because, if justified, it would not be true joy. Suffering, and certainly struggle, may be necessary for true joy to be possible at all. But struggle is possibility in action; we do not struggle in order to achieve a possibility, but the struggle itself is the actual making-possible of both loss and gain, victory and defeat.

That my present joy may require the affirmation of an ignominious and painful past is somewhat mysterious in a paradoxical sort of way. That struggle itself makes possible both defeat and victory rather than the other way around is also mysterious, because the order seems backwards to causal linkage. But what is not mysterious is that such possibility is in the concrete and not in the abstract. What could be more concretely possible than struggle itself? When truth is at stake, is not struggle as concrete possibility fundamental asking? We could not ask about ourselves without our own access to our own possibility, even if I must affirm a past horror in order to be joyous. In this way, the possibility becomes my own, and as such is concrete; as concrete it alone opens a way to fundamental asking. "What is man," that *we* art mindful of him?

3

Hearing

We ask only as we can speak; and ask fundamentally only from the loftiest reaches of language. If the actual as possible represents the state of our suspension between necessity and nothingness, it is language that connects them by hearing the call from both above and beneath. We cannot speak if we cannot listen; it is noise, not silence, that deafens. The supreme hush of reverential listening alone prepares us to ask fundamentally; it is what we as speakers hear, and not merely what we say, that links the distant to the intimate. We hear the psalmist ask, and in hearing, we learn to ask, too.

The great approach us in shadowed, silent places, like a secret wood or a darkened alley, and whisper as we listen. How did the sun rise?

> I'll tell you how the sun rose—
> A Ribbon at a time—

Emily Dickinson's poem (#318, Johnson) does not strictly ask the question, but imbeds it in the first line, as if we had just asked it. What astonishes us is why it should matter: *how* the sun rose? Who else asks quite this way? Her poem convinces us the question is worthy. We must hear her ask, even indirectly, as we hear David ask, or Kant, or Hamlet asking about to be or not to be. Unexpectedly, then, the inquiry into the language of asking begins by asking what it means to hear; and specifically, we listen to asking.

What do we hear when listening to asking that we do not hear from other forms of speech? We do not hear merely what the child asks, but the vulnerable, eager, opening that is a child's essence. We do not consider Hamlet's question only, but Hamlet questioning, which echoes the greatness of his confrontation. In this species of hearing we are snagged, as a fish by the hook, forced to face a possibility we perhaps had as lief left unconsidered. Language here spins a web that leaves us rapt; for unlike listening to thunder or to claims, listening to asking forces us to ask as well. I need not make a claim when another claims, nor curse when others curse, nor praise when others praise; but when I attend to asking I find myself asking, too. What, then, do I hear? Not all hearing is the same. The armed sentinel barks, "Who goes there?" We hear a demand in the form of a question. Not to answer may get us shot. "When do you close?" is a request for information; we hear in order to inform. Our role as answerer comes not into play at all; a sign on the door serves just as well. "How do these fit together?" We hear a puzzle: something that does not lack pieces, but lacks the locating, the coherence—the solution is there if we can but interlock them aright. "Should the press have no restraints at all in a free society?" We hear, not a puzzle, but a problem. There are judgments here, and compromise—complete satisfaction eludes us precisely because, as free, we recognize validity to restraint and unrestraint. Yet in confronting problems a far deeper level of thinking is required than in confronting puzzles. There are no algorithms; and to rely on thoughtful, experiential judgment nears the wholeness of the human response. To hear a problem raised provokes serious thinking.

These first four ways to hear may be in response to questions. They do not include the loftiest hearing, however, which is always an asking. We hear Dickinson's or David's or Plato's asking and we hear ourselves listening. To turn away from this asking is to turn away from ourselves. Although the first four questions are here posed in language, it is not obvious that language is really needed. Certainly I can demand and inform and puzzle without using words; and though it is unlikely, perhaps I may even be able to confront problems without them; but I could never ask fundamentally except through language, and indeed language at its highest level—language that reveals what it means to speak and hear as well as to confront. The danger is that we may rank these ways of hearing solely in terms of their topics, as if asking when the store closes is heard as seeking information because time and closings matter to our convenience, whereas the topics raised by Plato and David are more "profound." This danger must be resisted. It is not only the topic but how we hear that matters. We hear Dickinson's asking more fundamentally than an instructor's asking to paraphrase Descartes's proof for God's existence. As topics, God's existence or nonexistence may seem loftier than how to watch a sun rise; but how we hear the poet's asking is nobler than how we hear the classroom's analysis of the Fifth Meditation; unless, of course, the professor is truly gifted.

When we hear the sentry's challenge, we become a threat; when we hear the customer's question, we become a resource of information; when we hear the puzzle we become a calculator; when we hear the problem we become a reasoner; but when we hear Dickinson's profound asking, we become a co-asking, self-reflective thinker. For language to be language it must be heard; but we now discover that not all hearing is the same. Fundamental asking depends on language, and hearing fundamental asking differs from other ways of hearing. It is not simply the topic that determines fundamental hearing, but the power of language to entrap us into the web of asking. To hear, such that, in hearing, we ask, is the rarest phenomenon of language as truth-revealing.

Language as heard is truer to itself than as spoken, for we speak so that we might hear. Heeded hearing is listening, and when this listening lures us into asking, truth emerges just because truth is heard. It may seem trivial to ask how the sun rises; but to hear this asking in the language of Dickinson is to heed the truth that surprises: it now does matter how the sun rises, for we learn to see in its rising what it means for there to be an arriving sun and a new day with hope and promise, that opens with it. In this reflection a critical insight reveals itself. The hearing of fundamental asking in Dickinson's poetry links the phenomenon of the sunrise with what it means for the sun to rise and hence what it means to take joy in hoping. Such asking being heard and heeded, links what is to what it means. What it means for the sun to rise cannot be learned merely by seeing it happen, but by hearing the poet ask. The suggestion here is that such hearing is the truest access to language, and that such hearing already asks. This last point may seem counter-intuitive: hearing itself does not ask, they say; we hear *what* is asked. This objection is valid in the first four kinds of questioning, perhaps; but not in the fifth; for in fundamental asking what we hear itself provokes asking.

Language as hearing links meaning to things and events, and only in such linking is there truth. But language as hearing at the highest level is fundamental asking. To be or not to be, when heard, is asked; and to ask it is to make being itself meaningful precisely because it is asked about. What cannot be asked about cannot make sense. Until the profound is profoundly asked it is not profound at all. To this is now added: only when the profound is profoundly heard, can it be asked. Perhaps, indeed, great poets and great thinkers, themselves firstly hear before they speak. The analysis need not rely on the truth of this suggestion, however; for what goes on in the head of the poet cannot ever be of primary interest, even to the poet. It is not the soil, but the flower that emerges from it, that matters—for those who like flowers.

Language has always been among the greatest of philosophical interests; but questioning and asking are usually considered as poor, distant cousins to the apparent firstborn declarative sentence. Even if questioning or asking is grudgingly included in the family snapshots, it is usually posed in propositional form, like uncomfortable Sunday attire, that abrades the neck. The question, as a proposition, is dutifully clothed as an entity, there on the page of the album along with other sentences, outranked and outclassed by the putative heirs apparent to the title. Even if the cameraman is bold enough to forego the formality of the straitjacket of propositional attire, focus is placed, if not on the grammatic interrogative, on the questioner. It is thus thrice rebellious to suggest that, in daring to shift the focus away from declarative sentences, it is neither the question as a proposition nor even the questioner as interrogator, but the hearer of asking who is the truly firstborn of the language family. It is this authentic heir apparent who takes the picture, time-setting the camera to allow himself to be snapped as well. Once developed, what does this family portrait reveal?

> What's Hecuba to him or he to Hecuba
> That he should weep for her? . . .
> (Act II, S. 2)

Hamlet asks how a mere player, in a fiction, should be so moved by his own speech that he weeps; whereas he, the prince of Denmark, has full cause to weep, but cannot. Yet, at the end of this soliloquy, he recognizes the power of the play on the audience may well reveal Claudius as regicide. Hamlet seems to raise only a simple question concerning the chief player's vulnerability to sentimentality; but the question deepens to the anguish of his own hesitancy to act; and then becomes a profound questioning about art's relation to reality and the crushing duty to the unavenged. Hamlet's asking cannot be reduced to a single question, nor is it merely the cumulation of many questions; nor is it a series of ever-deepening questions, as if the last were the best. His questioning becomes an asking not at the end, but throughout, because the various questions themselves unfold as the profound asking of Hamlet's anguish. But it is our hearing of it that matters, just as it is Claudius's hearing of the play that will indict him. What do we hear?

We hear in this soliloquy, first, "Is it not monstrous . . . ?" The question itself provokes as asking. Why should the player's sentiment itself be *monstrous*? We hear more. It is not monstrous that the player should weep, but that Hamlet should not. Still, *monstrous* is a big word; hearing it, in the form of a question, reveals the awe inherent in our learning, as we hear, that what seems trivial is in fact truly monstrous. The monstrosity is not merely that Hamlet cannot weep, but that he cannot act; that a brother may have killed a king. Not avenging seems worse, more monstrous, than the murder itself. "Am I a coward?" the prince asks; we know that is not true, but we hear the torment in Hamlet's wondering if it be true. It is in our hearing his torment that we realize how ponderous the guilt and opprobrium on Hamlet is. He confronts the great paradox of evil: that evil itself is "monstrous." Yet, being monstrous, it seems beyond our capacity to avenge. This is Hamlet's true anguish; the real reason for his hesitancy. "What's Hecuba to him?" confronts us with "What is a king's fraternal murderer to the king's son?" To hear this—even though it may be "only" a play that we hear, not a real prince failing to avenge a real king—is to confront fundamentally by asking with the asking prince. It is little wonder that shortly after, we hear him ask: to be or not to be. We hear this, and we ask what it means to be at all. What is the worth of being if I am demanded to do that which I cannot do?

The fundamental asking that is heard in *Hamlet* is not restricted only to those moments when the text contains a question mark. The whole play asks, which is not to say that every scene interrogates. "What's Hecuba?" in the play becomes fundamental asking because in it we hear the parallel to Hamlet asking about Hamlet—What is a son to a murdered father?— and thus we also hear what it means for anything, even being itself, to matter at all.

If language is essential for fundamental asking then there must be more to language than communication. Granted some uses of language do communicate. (Communicate what? Ideas? But ideas need language in order to be *thought* before they are communicated.) It does not follow that all language is merely communication; perhaps it is not even principally communication. Fine language makes possible the realm of thinking in which what it means to confront our own existence is brought forth. This bringing-forth is asking. However, the phrase *fine language* is dangerous if left unqualified: strictly we should say "the hearing of fine language, finely heard, brings forth—asks—existence to be confronted." What amazes is not what Hamlet finally does, but how hearing the play confronts the audience with such surprising questions, questions that are not merely heard—recalling the etymology of *audience*—but in being heard, are asked. Hamlet's asking is what makes it so great a play.

We hear. We hear many things, we say, besides hearing language: the hissing, tumbling sea, the rattling truck, the sigh of the wind, the beat of the heart, and spoken words. Naming these things of course reveals that in hearing them as the sea, the truck, the wind, the heart, the word, language speaks in the hearing of them. Some suggest that what we hear in each case is merely noise, which then is "interpreted" as belonging to or coming from the sea and the truck. This is backward, since *noise* is an abstraction, while seas are real. What we hear as the sea is not first an abstraction—noise—which we later identify by naming it the sea. We also hear our own hearing, which is not an abstraction but a refinement, called asking. When, among other things like trucks and the wind, we hear words, we may falsely assume that this is the first occurrence of language. To have heard the sea as sea already is language. It is language that allows us to hear the sea. We may often hear things that confuse us, or that we do not know how to identify more precisely, or even that we have not heard before; but these are simply the unidentified or the unnamed; they are meaningful precisely because they await the naming sacrament—not because they are prelinguistic, heard entities. To hear them is to name them, even if the name is not yet announced or known. To hear the unidentified entreats the asking of what it is.

Hearing what is as yet unidentified now reveals itself as unexpectedly paramount. We hear the strange; and this very strangeness as a part of hearing shows itself as asking; but what is even more important is that the tug of war between the strange and the familiar originates language. Briefly, language occurs as speaking and hearing; the latter is existentially, though perhaps not always temporally, prior to the former: we hear, and then speak. Hearing gathers the familiar and the strange; we hear the distant in terms of its nearing; speaking, in response to this hearing, brings near what is distant, by articulating this gathering first as asking. Only the well-asked, the profoundly thought as asking, can elicit a response. The refined response, in turn, reveals the worth of the asking, and hence is dependent on it. We do not realize how important "What's Hecuba?" is until we hear this asking reach the splendor of the whole speech, and the speech the whole play.

What it means to hear is thus revealed as the true origin of language in which the pull between the familiar and the strange is its essence. Prose seeks to make the strange familiar; poetry seeks to make the familiar, strange. From hearing we proceed to asking and from asking to saying. Saying, at its most successful level, sanctions the asking and thereby reaches back into hearing.

With this sketch now laid out, it is necessary to step back and resurvey. The opening sentence of Aristotle's *Metaphysics* informs us that "All men by nature desire to know." It is thus not our knowledge that characterizes us but our desire for it. There is, if you will, *avidity* in our consciousness that must precede and perhaps exceed our grasp of it. We may contrast this with Kant's account: one way we are conscious, perhaps even the "first" way we are conscious, is to be receptive. The faculty of receptivity Kant calls sensibility. The German term for faculty is *Vermögen*—something that makes possible. If we listen to Kant carefully, however, we hear that this making-possible of our receptivity—the faculty of sensibility—is not passive, but active, which puts Kant closer to Aristotle. Sensibility contains the imagination: it projects forth its power to receive. Like a net being thrown out over the waters to snare the fish, the power (*Vermögen*) of receptivity actively projects outward; it is not like Huck Finn napping under a tree at the river's edge with a line tied to his toe, simply waiting for the fish to bite. The professional fisherman is not at leisure but at work, and work is active; Kant insists we make receptivity *happen*. For him, judgment and thinking are acts. Both Kant and Aristotle, however, are interested in accounting for knowledge, and hence they hurry past these exciting beginnings in which active asking or seeking must precede the accumulation of structured perceptions. Nevertheless, their wisdom is greater than their interests, and a close reading of them reveals their profundity. If the power to receive, sensibility, is projective, however, we must ask how this avidity, this restlessness of an uneasy consciousness, applies to hearing. Hearing as asking just is—the avidity to receive meaning.

Consider how we listen to an exciting question unfold. The very rules of grammar and syntax provide a fundamental guidance: we cannot hear what violates these limits, though we may notice it. What we long for is not new information, nor even "new" ways of linking items together as a puzzler does, but what is meaningful about ourselves as listeners to language. Juliet, hearing a voice from the garden below her balcony, says, "My ears have not yet drunk a hundred words / Of that tongue's utterance, yet I know the sound" (II, 2). The suggestion is that having drunk of this intoxicant, like a heady wine, she must ask, "Art thou not Romeo, and a Montague?"

There is eagerness in that simple verb, *drunk;* it hints at the inebriate. This entire balcony scene itself is drunk with names, words, sayings, tongues, hearing ("had I it written, I would tear the word"). It is the avidity, however, that in its huge, erotic passion discloses only to the listener the essential, truth-revealing deceit. These wonderful young lovers simply deceive themselves—and more importantly, deceive us the audience into believing what they say even though we know they cannot overcome their names. "What's in a name?" she asks; and we ask that, too, and foolishly, if wonderfully, believe names do not matter; but the play shows all of us are wrong. The mere names, Montague and Capulet, defeat the success of their passion; names do matter. Is our avidity as listeners then itself a deceit? No. We learn, painfully, the greater truth: we cannot gainsay their passion even if it does lead to death. Learning this through hearing shows us what true hearing, as projective receptivity, means. It is not by accident that one of the most intense passages on love in all of human literature should celebrate the metaphors and similes of names, words, and language. The passionate hear.

To define fundamental asking as the avidity to receive meaning is deeply paradoxical, for avidity seems active and receptivity seems passive. How can there *be* an "avid" receptivity? It is noted above that language "originates" in the tug of war between the strange and the familiar; here the avidity is, as poetic, to make the familiar strange, and in so doing, to bring the strange near to the familiar. Yet, the strange must always remain elusive, and the familiar must still ache for it, in order for fundamental asking to occur.

The discovery now is that meaning itself can never be some static object or referent, or even purpose. Meaning is the thinkability of that which is avidly asked. Whatever it is that allows or even demands fundamental asking is the avidly unsettled essence or meaning which makes possible or grounds thinking. What is deeply thought, therefore, is meaning; and if it is fundamental thinking (in the form of asking) it is of essential meaning, or simply the essence. What we ask about in fundamental asking is the essence: that which allows—or even compels—us to *think* about it. It is only now possible to suggest a hesitant and even reluctant signification to the phrase *fundamental asking* which has been used throughout: it is asking about essences, or essential meanings. Essence itself is seen as that which provokes asking in an authoritative way; essence makes possible thinking. To hear is to submit to this possibility. When we listen carefully we submit, as a lover submits to the beloved's passion or the thinker submits to both the beauty and authority of truth, or a patriotic citizen submits to the cruel call of his country.

This submission is made obvious by its counterpart: mishearing. We often hear only what we expect; or worse, what we want to hear. We violate true asking by preferring answered questions, thereby refusing to hear beyond what we already know. An original thinker's greatest foe is not the uninformed but the colleague who insists on reducing what is truth-seeking to what conforms to mere puzzle-solving—an insult that burns like treachery. Who, on hearing Dickinson's depiction of "Gazing Grain" is not tempted to mishear "grazing"; for what could it mean for the grain itself to *gaze*? We mishear Wagner as blaring and pompous if we do not hear his delicate counterpoint; we mishear the contrite as the whiner; the gentle as the weak. To avoid mishearing we must learn truly to listen; and this may take a lifetime to achieve. Submission as necessary for true hearing echoes back to Kant's depiction of sensibility as receptivity. It is not the supine or cowardly who submit; it is rather the passionate and the pious. To ask is to enable receiving—receptivity—and receiving endures, as the loyal miscreant endures due punishment. It takes courage to submit; it can be cowardly to mishear. Poets and philosophers are strange enough to be often misheard. Words are the spies of truth which the poet tortures to reveal their secrets; we the hearers submit to this torture in creative receptivity. Perhaps it is the philosopher who tortures questions to reveal their secrets; the instrument of such torture is in both cases language, not as spoken but as submissive hearing, the fundament of asking.

One of the greatest samples of true asking, and one that is modernly misheard, is the famous passage from Plato's *Meno* in which Socrates' interrogation of the slave-boy eases the paradox of inquiry. Meno, often depicted—by those more familiar with analyzing concepts than appreciating drama—as a species of philosophic arch-villainy, asks a truly disturbing question about asking. If knowledge must be assumed in order to ask, and if asking seeks knowledge, then we first must know before we can seek to know, which seems to make asking redundant. A slave-boy, who had never been "taught" geometry is asked about certain geometric relationships in figures drawn in the sand. The boy's ability to arrive at the right answer suggests there is a sense he "already" knew them, which gives rise to the suggestion that perhaps all knowledge is recollection. The mishearing British epistemologists find in this a clumsy but curiously effective argument for a priori knowledge, and the contrast between rational (innate) knowledge which cannot be taught, and empirical, sense knowledge which can only be experienced. It is, however, Socrates' task to show how questioning works; for it is only adroit, perhaps even inspired, asking that leads the boy to discover not only what the geometry answer is, but that he *knows* the answer with certainty: he knows that he knows. The boy answers the easy question correctly, but responds erroneously to the more challenging, second one. By persistent questioning, however, he realizes his mistake; and eventually is able to answer the third puzzle by pointing out the correct line, though since it is not a whole number he cannot name it. After this, Socrates claims the boy has true opinions within him, as if he had lived prior to human existence, for from what other source could he have gotten it? What is in his mind (a priori) therefore, is not knowledge but merely right opinion: it takes the educator (asker), Socrates, to bring these out, not a teacher who puts them in, before knowledge can be attained.

This passage, however, cannot be taken out of the dialogue, nor can this dialogue be taken out of the series that turns on Socrates' death and the revisitation of the whole series in the *Republic*. The *Meno* begins, unlike any other dialogue, starkly, with the troubling problem: Is virtue teachable? Socrates' hypothetical suggestion that perhaps virtue is like geometry, recollected, quite rightly incurs the wrath of Anytus, who enters the discussion at its crucial moment. His anger is critical; for if knowledge of the virtues can be recollected through the evocation by skilled askers, then the polis of Athens is not necessary. Anyone, Greek or non-Greek, can reach into his "memory" to find all the moral wisdom necessary for living the best of lives. Piety, however, suggests that loyalty to Athens is necessary for the best life. Is not the Socratic hypothesis impious? The *Meno* must give way to the *Euthyphro*. To ask if virtue be teachable is to confront the limits of piety.

Socrates is not above the fray, as the condescending hagiographers would have it, but is deeply agonized by it. His confrontation with Euthyphro is direct, honest, and terrible: "Am I impious?" Is not philosophy necessarily impious, seeking truths beyond any culture? It is only the *Republic* that embraces this with the counter-suggestion: it is *only* as pious that true inquiry can take place; only in the concrete culture, in the possibility within the actual. The piety of asking, however, deserves its own chapter; for the present moment the import must be placed on Socratic asking and our hearing it.

It is not outrageous to suggest that what it means for us to hear the dialogue is to be caught up in its thinking. We ourselves can work out the geometry at the same time as we hear the method at work; the entrance of Anytus is scary, which provokes the deeper meaning behind the slave-boy's "recollection"; it is a challenge to the moral authority of the polis. We realize the opening question is not answered but more deeply asked when

Socrates points out the two hypotheses, both in terms of their presuppositions and their seeming incoherent consequences. (A hypothesis, Socrates notes, is simply that which follows an *if;* but *if* itself is a mode of asking.) If virtue were teachable, good men would always have good sons, which is not the case. If virtue is knowledge, it would be recollected, which seems impious, for the polis is no longer needed. It is the putative teachability of virtue that eventually leads Socrates to his agonizing self-criticisms and ultimate death, for if virtue were not teachable the charge of impiety would make no sense at all, for Socrates would then be accused of doing the impossible.

In one sense, the seeming paradox in Meno's famous question is the easiest to resolve. How can we inquire, he asks, if we must both know and not-know in order to ask? The question answers itself. We know something but not everything, about any given topic. It is the suspense, the dialectical tension between knowledge and ignorance that allows us to ask. That this suspension becomes real suspense reveals the dramaturgy of the dialogue; when it threatens our lives as well as our trust in reasoning itself, the fundamental worth of such questioning becomes dramatic. We hear the dialogue avidly; our receptivity bares its teeth; this is courageous listening, as far from greenhouse academics as can possibly be imagined. Dialogue, etymologically, means "through language," *dia-legein;* we approach truth only through language. This language, however, is guided by essential asking. Questions are not posed merely as charming invitations to the honored guest, the answer; it is the asking that digs, reveals, terrifies confronts and re-asks. Mishearing the dialectic as a carriage of doctrine is simply folly. Answers serve questions, and servers rank below the served; both serve truth, which is the true sovereign, but asking is the firstborn and heir apparent of this king. To hear the asking, and not merely the several questions, in the dialogue is thinking at the highest level.

These brief visitations with Hamlet and Socrates reveal that fundamental asking is not reducible to any interrogative sentence, but relies on the broadest range of language. Even if we accept this, however, we yet wonder how it is that language allows us to ask the great questions. An analogy may help. I could study the bricks and mortar, the steel and glass, the pillars and beams that make up a great cathedral, and never get at its essence. Somehow, what I learn from these elements distracts from what I must see. Though these elements are needed to make the building, they do not "ask" the building. The architect's vision, concretized in the edifice itself, alone can provide this more ample, asking vision. Do I "see" the architecture? Surely I can, but not in the same sense I see the bricks and stone. It may be that I learn to see the architecture only after considering and reflecting, with what might be called avid receptivity. I am entirely misled if I seek merely to find the historical patterns of influence, or to find the proper label that types the work. If the building, as cathedral, reveals something of what it means to worship, though, I see the architecture as revealing the essence of the cathedral as the "place" of worship. It is ridiculous to deny we "see" architecture; but it is equally silly to attempt to see it by looking at bricks, steel, and stone. If I see the edifice *as* a cathedral, in which worship is made possible, I see fundamentally—which is not reachable either through the elements of the history or architectural theory. The kind of "seeing" that allows us to see architecture rather than mere buildings, itself is impossible without language, since the *as* itself asks. This fundamental seeing, in which the architecture matters, is akin to fundamental hearing, in which the asking matters. What does it mean to "see" as the architect sees; or as the avid receptor of the architecture learns to see? What does it mean to ask, as David or Plato or Kant asks, or as the avid hearer of this great asking learns to ask? Architecture reveals what it means to dwell, language, when heard reveals what it means to ask, and we can also ask what it means to dwell. This analogy cannot be pressed too far; the point of it is that no study of the elements that make up a building can ever provide its architecture, as no mere study of words or sentences can ever give us language that provides asking or essential meaning.

The prior chapter provides the existential meaning of possibility as the modal basis of asking, and with this the discovery of suspension. If we are hung between the extremes of necessity and impossibility, we are both parted and yet somehow connected between these extremes. We hear the lure of both, which makes hearing the link, as Hamlet's asking about being and not being confronts the tortured finitude of seemingly unanswerable duty. Language, then, is required for the suspense of being less than the angels but having dominion over the beasts; but it is not language as communication or command or even puzzling—it is language as hearing and asking.

Suppose we hear "What is our purpose?" and by this hearing we ask, thereby confronting ourselves in what we deem a fundamental manner. We then hear, either as a dim whisper from within our own asking, or from another's thinking, "Is this the proper question?" To have a purpose is to be subservient to some broader scheme. Chairs and microwaves have purpose, and were the purpose to be thwarted, they would be useless, and as useless, they have no worth at all. To ask for our purpose, then, misleads dreadfully: I do not have a purpose, I have meaning; nor do I have a value, I have worth. The asking deepens, and in deepening we have learned greatly. But the fact that we were originally misled on this lofty level of inquiry disturbs. How do we account for this? In asking for our purpose were we really not asking fundamentally? We may now realize the asking misleads, but when we heard it originally it seemed profound, fundamental, awesome. Having been misled, do we despair?

Asking for our purpose is still fundamental, not because it is the right way to ask, for it turns out to be dangerously distractive, but because from it we learn to deepen our asking. Errors that can be checked are not impediments to learning. It may be we must first ask seriously what our purpose is to discover we have none—indeed asking for our purpose shows we cannot have a purpose, since such asking is impossible for one designed solely to be useful. If learning we have no useful purpose leaves us with the bitter taste of nihilistic ash in our mouths, such desperation may be a necessary propaedeutic to digging more deeply to confound the apparent nihilism. The slave-boy, considering a far less serious question, first had to be confounded by his error before he could progress to more sophisticated geometric thinking. Fundamental asking does not depend on asking, almost by instinct, the right form of the question. Hypotheses, after all, are meaningful only because in some way they are testable, even if only in their negative consequence. (Disjunctive syllogisms, followed by hypothetical syllogisms of each disjunct, followed by *modus tollens*, is still one of the most revealing and fundamental procedures of logical analysis. Why should this surprise us?) To learn, even if by consequentialist reduction, that we have erred, is still learning. To discover I can ask wrongly even on the fundamental level does not invalidate such asking but sanctions it. Would we really prefer not to learn we have erred? Hearing fundamental asking is in itself no guarantee we have either heard or asked aright. Its correctness is not what makes it fundamental, nor its form, nor its topic. The inability to reduce architecture to the elements that make up the building does not invalidate architecture; neither does my original failure to grasp the architect's genius mean I cannot learn to see it; nor does this dependence on sensitivity to what it means to dwell render the learning a mere species of subjectivist appraisal. Architecture can, but need not always, be seen; but it is in either case the essence of the building; though not all architecture succeeds at this, and even the greatest may be flawed. Truth, revealed in hearing what is fundamentally asked, is there, too, even if misheard or poorly asked.

It is not obvious that asking for our purpose should be characterized as wrongly asked, since it may well be a necessary testing of a shaky hypothesis that is not so much false as unrefined. Even great architectural masterpieces may yet be seriously flawed; but a flawed masterpiece is still a masterpiece, in any field, and is far worthier than unflawed but unmasterful achievement. There can be no algorithm deciding which questions or problems constitute fundamental asking, any more than there can be rules dictating how to compose greatly. We still can hear the fundamentality in some asking, however, just as we can see architectural genius in a great building. It is there to see for those who can learn to see it; fundamental asking is there to be heard by those willing to hear.

4

Surprise

It is surprising that we are the only species that surprises itself. Mice and weasels can be startled, frightened, and roused; and curiosity can lead to dangers that panic chipmunks. We alone surprise ourselves simply by discovering ourselves. Why is this? Are our expectations always so banal? Thunder startles, outrages shock, the unexpected stuns, the prodigious amazes—but what surprises is that we can ask, and even ask what it means to ask. The unsurprised do not ask. Asking itself surprises; and in both senses: that we can ask at all is surprising; and being able to surprise ourselves and to be surprised by ourselves is essential for asking. Love surprises; but for the oft-rejected, being loved surprises more. We are surprised by the utmost depravity of our kind or even of ourselves, and likewise surprised by the beauty we create and the triumphs we achieve; though since we are the authors of both the repulsive and the ennobling it is not clear why either or each should surprise; but it does.

It may appear that what surprises is the suddenly unfamiliar, like finding a reptile in the bathtub; but this is surprise only in the sense of being startled or even frightened by the unexpected. What might be called *existential surprise* is curiously not of the strange but of the most intimately familiar, wrenched from comfortable belonging into breath-snatching self-discovery. Those bored by life need only imperil it to find it precious; the time-worn friendship exposes surprising ligatures of adhesion when distanced; the forgotten duty binds with unexpected, raw authority. How do we account for our surprise at learning ourselves? *Gnostho sauton* proclaims the Oracle at Delphi, "know thyself"; and Socrates took this deeply to heart. How could we possibly *not* know ourselves? That we might be surprised by self-discovery is itself surprising; and as a surprise, it opens up inquiry. The strangeness of the strange is unsurprising since we expect the alien to be other; the strangeness of ourselves is entirely unexpected, and hence the most familiar surprises most. Indeed it is the very familiarity of the familiar that surprises.

Many philosophers have noted this in various ways. Aristotle says philosophy originates in wonder; Kant opens the *Critique of Pure Reason* by pointing out the "peculiar fate" that haunts and thralls the mind with legitimate questions which it cannot entirely resolve. That we do not even know the meaning of our existence Nietzsche finds as a huge joke on us that only the learning of the superman can redeem. But jokes are surprises that wryly make us laugh at ourselves by revealing ourselves. It is the comic dramatist, the poet, and above all the philosopher who, after years of refinement and struggle discover surprise; the neophyte is too raw, too eager, too serious, to be self-surprised. When all is new nothing surprises; which is why children and innocence should never be the paradigms of wonder. In order to be surprised we must first be familiar with ourselves; the comfort of belonging establishes a local piety, outside of which is the unsurprising strange. If we are told that aliens procreate only in dutiful pain, that their children are ugly whilst the aged are beautiful, that only their health destroys, that sleep causes anxiety and torment calms, all this we can accept with aplomb since the different ought to be different. Only if the strangely alien are shown to be exactly like us might we be surprised.

The Delphic imperative troubles us because of its surprising assumption that most of us, for the most part, do not know ourselves, and so we must ask about this strange ignorance and how it is possible. The modal nature of such possibility has already been shown: it is the possibility within the actual, located in the avid receptivity of meaning; it is brought forth to us in language as hearing. Being possible as actual can be heard precisely and only because of suspense, both in the spatial sense of being located between extremes, as David shows us in the psalm, and in the temporal sense of dramatic suspense heard in the unfolding of tragic destiny, as Sophocles shows us in *Oedipus*. Suspense creates surprise. Even in the more common artistry this prevails. The well-known, attractive film star is shown walking slowly down a creepy corridor, thunder rumbles, lightning flashes; creaking and snapping, moans and shadows all heighten suspense so that when the attack comes the impact is more vivid. Without these icons of suspense, the surprise would be less successful. Totally unprepared violence may startle us more; but it is an aesthetic curiosity that the more we "expect" the surprise the more surprising it is. Surprise does not originate in total ignorance followed by complete enlightenment; rather conscious ignorance, as a species of suspense, evokes a certain expectation—or listening—that is asking. What we listen for in such hearing is truth; and so truth is the ultimate surprise. (And this is why abstract theories by themselves, however revolutionary, do not surprise, for they need not be true.) Suspense, and being suspended, thus foster fundamental asking by enhancing surprise. It is not curiosity, irritation, simple ignorance, or casual interest that originates asking, but ourselves surprising ourselves. How do we surprise ourselves?

It may be thought that self-surprise is due merely to the enormous complexity of our neurological or psychological makeup. Consider this apparently satisfying account: dark and shameful desires lurk in the cesspool of barely contained urgings; only the stretched plastic wrap of civility keeps these redolent fumes from being inhaled, and the tiniest pinprick releases the toxic gas. Civility induces shame, and it is shame that covers the stench. Unvented, however, this membrane either pops with the buildup of steamy pressure, or so stifles the creative urges that the fierce appetites soon wither in unexercised atrophy. When these emissions from beneath leap or seep out, we are dazzled by the confusion. Some call this surprise, and take both alarm and satisfaction at its release. There is no need to deny that we do indeed clamp the lid of civility on the rank stew of dark urgings—every defender of order from the morning of civilization onward recognizes this—but such an account, though lurid, cannot explicate self-surprise. Any explanation of anything that depends on complexity to persuade its acceptance is moribund from the start; it is merely a species of the fallacy of ignorance. (Since you cannot grasp it, it must be true.) It is not complexity but simplicity that truly surprises. Our psychological makeup is doubtless complex, and that deep within us may lurk unholy wants and scary experiments is recognized by every adult who reflects at all. There is nothing new in this; but it cannot explain David's shift from the heavens to his asking about man.

If the suggestion above is to matter, and not be distracted by mantras about human complexity, then how we surprise ourselves should perhaps be approached from the phenomenon of suspense and its remarkable power to please. We *enjoy* suspense as well as the ignorance inherent in it. Prodigious box-office receipts from well-crafted thrillers show that even ordinary audiences delight in suspense. The more literate enjoy the more artful suspense of masterworks such as *Oedipus*. It is indeed one of the fundamental reasons why we educate people to become literate: the classroom struggles with Sophocles' text are amply justified when the performance of the play satisfies so deeply. This enjoyment of suspense, however, cannot be explained as an itch being appreciated because of the pleasure of the scratch. Rather, what pleases in suspense is being in suspense; we take no little satisfaction in this direct, felt modality of possibility concretized through letting surprise happen. This is not restricted merely to aesthetic experience, though it is most obvious there. We delight in taking risks, in gambling, in adventures, and in laughing—all of which require an embrace of suspense and surprise. We also seem to be able to take delight in deceiving others, as in a chess gambit, or in keeping secret a surprise party, or in outmaneuvering an enemy. Men take further delight in the magnificent mystery of a woman, loved in part because of her secrets. Lest we interpret these as mere methods for advantage, we reflect that many of these mysteries do not advantage of us except only as they suspend. We even put on masks that knowingly deceive ourselves, or at least keep secret ourselves from ourselves, as when we trust the beloved who is unworthy of trust or persist in graciousness when it is wasted on the ingrate, or suspend disbelief in the current of the fantastic, like watching opera. The clue here is that we can delight in suspense precisely because of the truth that we are in suspense. Truth matters, and if the truth be that we are suspended between "angels" and "beasts," such suspense entails our own self-discovery. But suspense, when properly understood, is already surprise. It is this suspenseful surprise that enables fundamental asking. Without suspense there is no true surprise; without true surprise there is no fundamental asking; and without fundamental asking there is no truth—at least, no truth in the sense of self-revealing; truth, that is, about ourselves.

Not all surprise enables asking; only self-surprise does, and the reason it does is in part because of suspense. Suspense is nothing other than the concrete phenomenon that enables our own actuality to be seen as possible. In suspense we do not abstractly conceive of theoretic possibility which then is tested by confirming experience, but palpably confront possibility as already belonging to our essence. It belongs to, as it enables, surprise—emphasizing now its etymology: *sur-*(super=above) *prendre* (to take)—we are *transported above* ourselves. Why, though, does this suspenseful surprise enable asking?

It is only when what surprises is our own reality—"heard" as concrete possibility, i.e., possibility within the actual, confronted by intensifying suspense—that asking must take place. This is not due merely to Aristotle's "desire to know" or reason's "peculiar fate" noted by Kant, or even Nietzsche's "joke"—though our ability to laugh at ourselves is perhaps closer than the other two. We ask, when self-surprised, as an existential necessity. These are not temporally distinct occasions that function as psychological causes; we do not "first" enjoy suspense, which then "causes" us to take surprise, which in turn "causes" us to ask about what is going on. The suspense is already a part of asking. Not to ask constitutes a retreat from our essence; unasked, our existence becomes unworthy of thought.

Asking is a species of thinking rooted in our ability to be surprised about ourselves. As a way of thinking there is a certain degree of authority in it, which is why it is an existential necessity. Just as the ordinary question "when" displays the wider range of the calendar, the clock, or history, which provides schematic structure that gives coherence and hence authority, so asking fundamentally necessitates the opening up of what was hidden—surprise—when what was hidden is fundamental essence. This is not some abstractly conceived taxonomic chart or scheme, but the concrete authority in our troubled suspension. We ask about the meaning of our existence precisely because the authority of truth can surprise; and we are surprised by this authority because of its arrest under the subpoena that suspends. We do not, then, ask in order to render the authority unsurprising, but to yield to it as surprise, just as we yield to legitimate arrests by officers of law, as enforcing.

In all surprise there is a certain yielding, as when the unexpected brilliance of a performance captivates us; but in self-surprise this captivity brings us before the more ample tribunals of our own self-judgment. However conceived, this tribunal is ultimate, like the Supreme Court: there is no further reality lurking beyond it to which the searcher can point as an explanation. To be caught up in the thrall of self-judgment, that is, to yield to it, is to ask. Since asking necessarily displays a structuring order or authority, the surprise is that such authority is found not in what we hear but in our hearing. How do we fit into the grander scheme of things? To *hear* this question in our own asking reveals its impropriety: unlike the rest of the world, the heavens and the stars and possibly even the angels and the beasts, we do not "fit" precisely because in asking where we fit we are no longer merely a part of the grander scheme. The asking changes who we are. To some extent we do indeed "fit," namely, the extent to which we are unsurprised. We fit as part of the food chain, as procreators of the species, as the capstone of evolution, as entities that begin as womb-extenders and end as corpses, destined for rot and other's fading memories. Having said all this, realizing it as true, we are then surprised to find that our asking is not accounted for by any of these naturalist schemes. We yield to whatever authority haunts beyond the perimeters of such schemes, and find ourselves surprised. What does it mean not to fit into any scheme, yet still recognize authority?

In his poem "The Sea and the Mirror," which asks about Shakespeare's *The Tempest*, W. H. Auden asks: "O what authority gives/Existence its surprise?" This poetic question is a tissue of marvels. The close juxtaposition of authority, existence, and surprise itself is richly suggestive, demanding our attention as worthy of the deepest thought. The fantastical, magical art of *The Tempest* provides us with this authority, but that there *be* authority in surprise at all is more astonishing. Why should surprise need authority? How do we understand the term *authority* if this poetic discovery be true? The etymology (*augere*) suggests origin, in the sense of making something happen; but even in its earliest English usage it entails a sense of right or power. We distinguish now between raw power and authority: a gunman demands our wallet by force, but the taxman demands his cut by the rightful authority of law. Yet, law does not make authority possible; it is rather authority that makes law possible. Governments pre-exist the laws they give; and even unhappy laws are obeyed out of respect for the authority that originates them. There is, then, something lawlike and originating in existential surprise. The authority of art to surprise is thus a paradox, for surprise violates the assumed and expected—the "grander schemes," if you will—which are normally thought as the law governed or regulated. It is not the regulative as ruled, but the universal as original, that authorizes the surprise. It is when art reveals to us our universality in ways that surprise that we are enrapt by its authority. It is the rare, exquisite love of Romeo and Juliet that shows us, surprisingly, the authority of the universal meaning lurking in all human love, however common or flawed. In this sense, authority comes from sheer excellence or refinement, and is approached through ideality, which is one of the fundamental ways we think. It is tempting then to say that it is Shakespeare's genius that establishes such perfection in his language that it takes on an authority to force us to learn what otherwise we could not. This learning surprises us because it shows a universality, and hence authority *over* us, in our own natures that we at best had only sensed vaguely, if at all.

There is, however, more to it. *The Tempest* is considered by some scholars to be Shakespeare's final play, in which Prospero represents the poet himself, doffing his magic mantle at play's end, giving a decided melancholy to the fantasy. We leave the isle of enchantment to return to the forgotten Dukedom of Milan, where tricksy boys like Ariel do not belong, and the rule of the right has no place for poetry or surprise. Is the island but a dream? Is art illusion? We leave the theater where wonders happen and ruefully trudge back to the flat, unwonderful world of everyday life. It is in many ways a harder play to endure than *Lear* or *Hamlet*. If the island is fantasy, and the exit from the theater is an entrance to reality, then it is not wonderful but disappointing. The surprise rests merely on deceit—pleasant deceit, to be sure, but still the stuff of dreams. There is some truth in the melancholy, but the magic, the fantasy, the dream still surprise *us;* and we are always, even when watching fantasy, real. It may be magic that rips us out of prosaic forgetfulness, but the truth learned from illusion is itself not illusion. That we may visit Prospero's island is yet wonderful, and this visitation persists in its bestowal of self-revelation. We do not, in asking fundamentally, step up to a naturalistic scheme, but step out of schemes altogether, to mirror ourselves to ourselves. Fantasy, as a rigorous, demanding, mature art form is as far from everyday fantasizing as can be imagined. That Prospero and Ariel can perform some magical wonders curiously leaves the discoveries all the more realistic. It is not, after all, that fine a place: Caliban lives there; Prospero must suffer the terrible ache of watching his beloved Miranda fall in love with Ferdinand; he must cruelly transform his brother's cruelty into respect; he harshly keeps the wonderboy Ariel in strange bondage, and must leave him only with greater suffering in his heart. The wonder is not in the uses of magic, but in the power to show us how to ask who we are.

When Auden profoundly notes the authority of *The Tempest* to give existence its surprise, he is not taking refuge in mere illusion. Fantasy, rather than naturalist schemes, may mirror the sea of our unfathomable mystery. It is Auden, not Shakespeare, that we hear asking now; and he asks a fundamental question. Art, as truth revealing, surprises; it is the truth that gives it authority. In hearing this authority in artistic surprise, we are enabled to discover in our actuality the concrete possibility that universalizes by suspending us between the lofty and the base; we are caught, by means of a storm, on an island of enchantment where magic and fantasy reveal nonmagical and nonfantastic truths we must confront.

The authority that gives existence its surprise—and hence its truth—is not restricted to the enchanted isles of art. Few discoveries surprise more deeply than the suspense inherent in Kant's antinomies. After hearing through supreme effort the analyses of the synthetic a priori, the forms of intuition, the categories and the schematism, we are led into a deep respect for the critical; but then to turn the page and see right before our eyes, without any preparation or warning, the surprising violence that reason wreaks upon reason, the powerful proofs for conflicting, ultimate claims about the universe, suspends us perforce between the need for final unity and the irresistible evidence from our own mind we can never get there. To one unfamiliar with the work, such a magical, fantastic tempest like the antinomies would never be expected from a fusty rigorist like Immanuel Kant. The mind surprises itself profoundly in such a maneuver. So do the frightening erotic dialogues of Plato. We do not need the feigning arts to produce suspense and the truth-revealing surprise that authorizes our asking.

Three important notions have been suggested by this chapter. The first is that what provokes asking is not mere curiosity, or an itch to resolve a puzzler, but self-surprise. The second is that such surprise is made possible by suspense, in both the temporal and spatial senses of the term. The third is that this suspense-surprise is authoritative. These three notions themselves already reveal much that is contained in asking; they are not mere psychological preparations that lead us to an entirely nonsurprising enablement called asking: surprise, suspense, and authority are essential parts of asking; we are already asking when suspenseful surprise manifests its authority.

5

Ordinary Questions

"What is it?"
"What do you mean?"
"I mean, is it animal, vegetable or mineral? or *what?*"

The first question is shown by the third to be coherent only in terms of some sense of what the answer might be. It need not be that animal, vegetable, and mineral exhaust the range of possible answers; but it does show that to ask what something is already presupposes what kind of answer would be acceptable. "This is a sponge; it has characteristics of both animal and vegetable." Or, "It's a spiritual reality, it's neither animal, vegetable, nor mineral." This latter response is made possible by the "or what?" We therefore need not know either directly or even specifically what categories or types contain all possible answers; but there is an authority that anchors questioning in a nonrandom, though "open," project of coherence. There are familiar interrogatives: *who, what, when, where, how, why, whether.* Each presupposes a certain way of being coherent: *why* seems to demand the coherence inherent in motive or purpose; *who* demands agency or persons; *what* asks for class identification; *when* demands time and its measure; *where* demands space and its measure; *how* demands efficient causality; *whether* demands options. One species of delinquency in questioning is to cross over from one to another: "In the drawer," cannot answer "When is she coming?" Yet, considerable confusion reigns when it seems one species of questioning can either be replaced or conjoined with another. "Why do flowers smell sweet?" may be answered in terms of *how* their emanations affect the nasal receptors. Some of these species may seem entirely reducible to another, at least in certain areas, as Darwin reduces the why to the how in biological phenomena. Do we know with certainty and in advance that all questions must occur under these familiar interrogatives?

Not all questioning uses interrogatives; simple grammatic inversion accomplishes genuine asking without them. "The relief column is coming" states; "Is the relief column coming?" asks. Is this grammatic convention a mere peculiarity of some languages, or does it suggest a profounder point: that questioning as dialectic proceeds in the opposite direction of declaratives linking by deductive inference. "All men are mortal, and Socrates is a man; so Socrates is mortal," states in the form of declarative sentences based on or linked by, deductive inference: "If I know that Socrates is a mortal because he is a man, what must I assume in order for this to be true? That all men are mortal." I can figure this out, too: but it is not deduction. The former inference asserts, the latter asks, but it is authoritative asking.

Arguments can be given suggesting that perhaps the various interrogatives are not irreducible. With Darwin in mind we might ask whether *why* is really *how;* with Einstein in mind we may wonder if *when* and *where* really are that distinct; perhaps with Newton in mind the *what* becomes the *how?* That these reductions *may* be the case must be emphasized; it is not obvious they *must* be the case; at the very least considerable argumentation seems required to justify such reductions; the burden of proof is on the reducer. Why do flowers smell? may not be answered by accounting for how they smell. We can suggest a purposive account, citing the techniques of floral propagation; or we can even ask why the sweetness of a flower should be granted to us as an undeserved boon. Merely because the "how" question can be asked of the flower's sweetness does not necessarily mean the other questions have lost their status.

Keen observers of human inquiry rightly note it is possible to be grossly misled by asking the wrong question; or that genius at times consists in discovering how to ask the right question. How do we discern the difference? After the fact, it is fairly easy to see earlier thinkers were misled by bad questioning, and then following a revolutionary breakthrough, succeed prodigiously by asking in the proper way; but such hindsight cannot provide algorithms for future asking. There are some occasions, as in Darwin's discoveries or Kant's antinomies, where the false asking reveals itself in rather spectacular ways: that is, the old way of asking, when pressed, shows itself to be either contradictory or incoherent, or perhaps even meaningless in a given context, thereby forcing a new way of questioning. But these moments are exceedingly rare. Far more frequently we find, for example, that a criminal investigator is so focused on who had the means and opportunity to commit the crime that he overlooks the motive. In such a case we might say by asking the "wrong" question he overlooked the one clue that best would resolve the crime. This is fairly banal, however; and the point may well be one, not of questioning, but of method; which prompts a further point: rigidity of method itself may be the culprit in rendering alternative forms of questioning unavailable, and thus frustrates successful inquiry. Having no method at all may be a form of interrogative anarchy; but predetermining method by abstract analysis may well produce interrogative despotism. There is no paradigmatic, flawless method which, if followed rigorously, can succeed in answering all questions, even within a limited field. Discoveries may well require new methods, and new methods may well reveal new questions or even new kinds of questions. Descartes's orgulous pretensions in the First Meditation are deeply offensive in this sense; but so too are contemporary claims about adherence to "the scientific method," as if there were only one, could be no other, and all agree what it is.

If there be no absolute method, neither can there be no single way of asking that is necessarily fundamental. We may ask, for example, "Why do we suffer?" or "Must we suffer?" noting that the latter form, not using an interrogative, but relying solely on grammatic inversion, seems a more flexible or open way to ask. "What does it mean to suffer?" is perhaps even better. "Is it necessarily in our nature to suffer?" is more precise, but carries what may be infelicitous baggage with the dubious term *nature*. These four ways of asking about suffering each seem able to ask about suffering in a fundamental way. There are perhaps arguments that can be given showing why one form is superior to the other; but the extended manner in which the responses are carried out would have to constitute a part of that argumentation. The results matter. These four, however, and perhaps other ingenious ways, are quite distinct from questions such as, "How do we suffer?" or "What causes suffering?" or even "Do we all suffer?" A depiction of neural endings activated by trauma may serve science very well but does not seem to have the same status as the first four. It is possible, in other words, that one could argue "Need we suffer?" is the best way to ask about suffering, but "What does it mean to celebrate?" is the best way to address celebration. There is nothing wrong in trying to address all major questions in one style of questioning; but the judgment whether such questioning is superior would have to await the actual inquiry itself. There is also nothing wrong with addressing each major question differently, for it is possible that one topic may yield more truth in one manner of questioning whereas a second topic would yield more truth addressed in another manner. Even so, we still seem to realize in advance that some forms of questioning cannot be fundamental: *when* we suffer is not as fundamental as what it *means* to suffer.

We speak of "raising" questions; but do not speak of "lowering" them. What does this metaphor suggest? Does it mean that questions lie dormant in the loam of possibility and then are roused by some sunlight of irritation or surprise? Or does the metaphor suggest lifting the question up, suspending it on a higher level than the answers? Perhaps it has a Micawber-like suggestion of trusting in future opportunities, so that questions, like "something," will "come up"? Or is it like raising children, fostering and nursing the juvenile interrogation until it reaches the maturity of the answer? Perhaps it is like raising the target: giving something to shoot at. Or do we speak of *raising* the way we raise our tonal inflection when we orally ask a question? By mere inflection, in which the final word or words are spoken on a higher, tonic scale, one can change a statement into a question: "I went to her house(?) . . ." The speaker invites a nod of recognition: "yes, I know what you mean: *her* house." By raising the pitch of the last two words, even though the sentence as written is still declarative, it interrogates or invites assent. Perhaps, then, "raising" a question comes about because of this oral convention. The most likely of these suggestions is that questions are always lurking as possibilities behind every claim or act of cognition; and that when we ask them we focus on which interrogation best enables thinking about them. "Raising" is thus a species of isolating or focus that enables inquiry. If this is so, questions, either implicit or explicit, enable thinking; perhaps they are necessary conditions for all and any reflective thinking.

We perceive an object. If we were to proceed further than perception— i.e., to think about what we perceive—we must, implicitly or explicitly ask a question: we must "project"—that is, "enable"—by means of the imagination, a scheme of coherence that makes the object thinkable, as clocks are projected as schemes that allow for identifying particular times of the day. Each of the interrogatives, as is noted above, has its own unique scheme. Kant identifies similar products of the imagination as "schemata"—that is, schemes that are isomorphic with, or possibly even rooted in, the laws of nature. It is not necessary to rely on Kantian authority here; but it is very helpful to recognize that schemata are not abstract possibilities but possibilities rooted in, as enabling, actuality. We do not idly—i.e., abstractly— speculate that sequential time is a possibility that just happens to correspond to the causal series. Rather, the concrete accounting of events by means of the causal scheme requires the projective enabling of temporal schemata. This enabling, as projective, is rooted in the imagination, and hence is a possibility, to be sure; but it is a possibility already and necessarily imbedded in the actual. The return of the Portuguese sailors with their log out of synch with the calendar requires that we think about a circling orb that itself can be circled—possibility within the actual—and not merely an abstract, though hugely convenient, convention like the dateline. (The dateline impedes, rather than enhances, thinking.)

If we then accept provisionally the Kantian language—and it must be stressed that we need not do this—we see there is a "faculty" that accounts for questions, namely, the faculty of the productive (not reproductive) imagination, projecting lawlike schemes (schemata) that provide coherence and hence thinkability. Without this faculty, questions would be impossible. Accordingly, the projects of coherence that lie behind the various questions, such as the coherence in motivation and purpose (why), agency or persons (who), time as measured (when), space as measured (where), causality as measured (how), types and tokens as measured taxonomically (what), and options as offered (whether), are the result of being able to imagine in accordance with laws; or, if the legalistic machinery of Kant's critique of the faculties seems too automatic or algorithmic, perhaps the term *law* should be replaced by *authority*. These "projects of coherence" have no direct analogue in Kant, of course—the only reason for mentioning him is simply that he insists the imagination can produce authoritative schemes, which are here presented as projects of coherence; they enable thinking. How do they work?

> *Orlando:* Very well. What would you?
> *Rosalind:* I pray you, what is't o'clock?
> *Orlando:* You should ask me what time o' day; there's no clock in
>   the forest.
>   —*As You Like It*, III, 2

This comic cleverness initiates Rosalind's wondrous discourse on the "divers paces" of time; but note first Orlando's subtle point. Without clocks you cannot ask about clocked time; but the clockless are not thereby bereft of any and all temporal measure. Mornings, evenings, nighttimes are still meaningful. Prior to clocks there could never be three o'clock, though what we call that now would still be a part of afternoon—assuming that "noon" is not 12:00 but simply the highest point of the sun's daily course. Orlando chides the "youth" for improper *asking*. Both clocked time and the day's simple divisions into earlier and later segments are schemes of coherence, that is, they allow for meaningful discourse about time. Clock time is simply more sophisticated than what Orlando calls "time o' day." Rosalind, though, discourses cleverly on what it *means* to be in time, noting that the same duration may seem too short for some—the thief on the way to the gallows—and far too long for others—the maid waiting for the promised wedding. Here the difference between patience, impatience, eagerness, and dread are given different concrete images of time as experienced; and this too is a "scheme," making coherent the distinctions we make between subjective assessments of time.

Coherence is achieved, in this case, by comparisons. And though we quite properly call these assessments "subjective," they are nonetheless universally recognized and nonarbitrary. The structure of coherence that measures time by the clock is one scheme; measuring time by the positions of the sun is another; that which allows us to distinguish patience from impatience is another. It were folly to insist these are interchangeable—that impatience always and only occurs after thirty-two minutes of delay. Yet both Orlando and Rosalind talk meaningfully about time.

Orlando's correction of Rosalind's asking shows us, however, that on some occasions it is possible to refine or reduce. Both Kant and Darwin argue that purposive accounts that ask *why* are inapplicable to nature; but neither thinker thereby infers that the question *why* is always in principle reducible to *how*. Leibniz makes an even more curious, brilliant, though dubious, assumption: he admits *why* and *how* rely on entirely different ways of thinking; but he suggests these questions are merely different perspectives of the same coherence—they are in harmony, indeed a nonachieved, hence "pre-established," a priori, harmony.

There are two fundamental concerns of reason: consistency and coherence. The former is essentially negative: we do not want to contradict ourselves; and so we seek both rules, as in logic, and procedures, as in making distinctions, to avoid inconsistency. Coherence seeks positively to bring things together, to integrate and interlock the pieces so as to bring unity to diversity. When there is an established or agreed-upon field of discourse, such coherence can be achieved by constructs, both concrete and abstract. These constructs, when projected by the imagination as forms establishing unity, may be called schemes of coherence. In the concrete, everyday world, palpable representations of these schemes include maps, Cartesian coordinates, clocks, calendars, computer hard-wiring, telephone menus, elevator buttons, rule books for games, military chains of command, striped parking lots, mirrors, and alphabetized indexes. With such devices a certain coherence is established; some of these are entirely conventional and pragmatic, others seem inevitable or even natural; so that the temporal divisions of night and day seem natural, division of the day into twenty-four hours seems conventional. In either case, however, when such divisions are used to interrelate parts, it is still a projected scheme of coherence, whether it be natural or conventional. Darkness succeeding light may be nothing more than natural phenomena; but when I project forward or backward into the coherence of sequentiality, I imagine a scheme which makes sense of the constancy inherent in such succession, and with this scheme measure, and hence achieve a coherence to, the temporal changing from night to day. The scheme brings night and day together, and hence makes them cohere. We achieve *consistency* by distinguishing night from day, for it cannot be both light and dark at the same time; but we achieve *coherence* only by the project of sequentiality, which links them together as a synthesis. Coherence thus does much more than consistency.

Ordinary questioning consists precisely in *raising* these schemes *as* schemes of connective synthesis before the mind, and not merely *using* the scheme to determine a specific item, providing answers. It is the questions that establish and determine the schemes and not the other way around; but answers presuppose the question-originating schemes, and hence are derived from them. Without the more original raising of ordinary questions there could be no coherence. There is, then, an understandable though misleading tendency to seek a superscheme which would serve as a paradigm for all questioning and hence all coherence. The traditional interrogatives, however, are, in ordinary usage, specific in their schemes of coherence, and hence as such could never provide the ultimate question. It is only when I ask without a scheme at all that I ask fundamentally; though this does not mean that fundamental asking cannot use traditional interrogatives. "Who am I?" may be a mere request for a name; or it could confront the meaning of my singular existence; or it could constitute the asking for what it means to be a person. In the first of these there is a scheme of coherence, as an actor asks which role among the drama's cast of characters he should play; in the last there is no scheme but a directly confronted reality, made available only by self-reflection. Reflection on how schemeless and hence fundamental asking turns on the asker as reality must await the subsequent chapters; the present focus is yet restricted to raising ordinary questions.

Insistence on the nonreducible integrity of each of the traditional interrogatives becomes perilous if pressed too far. Deep thinking, which may not always be fundamental thinking, may require considerable intermingling of questions. "Who am I?" may ask differently from "What am I?" and both may be distinct from "Why am I?"; but all three may be integrated in any serious attempt to come to grips with the mystery of our existence. The range of asking is always greater than the range of specific questions—as was noted in the variants of asking about time in *As You Like It*. Even in the most ordinary or banal asking, the specific interrogatives are multiple strands interwoven into a net cast onto ample waters. It is for this reason, in part, that the asking mystery titles the inquiry; it relucts to name a specific question.

Interrogation based on grammatic inversions is not immune from the need to project coherence. "Is the relief coming?" asks *whether* it is coming, and hence projects at the very least the coherence of options or disjunction. "Need we suffer?" strictly asks about modality: Is suffering necessary or contingent? But lurking behind this seemingly innocent question of modality is the more serious one: Why should innocent people suffer? and hence projects the coherence of purpose, intention, or possibly, meaning. The use of grammatic inversion as a way of asking may appeal just because it is less specific as to which of the traditional interrogatives best reveals how to project coherence. It is not suggested however that grammatic inversion need be a superior way of asking. It is simply one among various ways we *raise* schemes of coherence rather than using or relying on them to give answers.

Regardless of the scheme, however, every serious questioning presupposes as a part of its coherence the possibility of response. There is no guarantee that any question will be productive; but what the scheme provides in its coherence is the possibility of truth. This is not incidental to questioning; it is essential. Unless we are playing games or relying solely on rhetoric, we ask, not for any answer, but for the right answer, even though it need not be forthcoming. What is more spectacular than that truth is essential for questioning is the converse: questioning is essential for truth. We do not, outside of games, ask to be deceived, so that inherent in our basic understanding of asking even ordinary questions is that truth matters. Coherence may not be the essence of truth, but it certainly is a necessary condition for it; and coherence as is noted above is far more than mere consistency. Ordinary questions, however, do not merely project schemes of coherence; they do so in a way that evokes discrimination between the false and the true. I ask questions, both ordinarily and fundamentally, because truth matters—a point that may seem obvious; but if I do, then truth itself must be essentially already constitutive of any and all possible questioning.

"It's on the right," is as a naked utterance, bare of any meaning; and is thus neither true nor false. The incoherence of this utterance, however, is not due solely to the vagueness and ambiguity of its referents; but rests also on its exile from the parental origin of the implicit or explicit prior interrogation. Looking south from atop the Empire State building, I ask where the Statue of Liberty is. The response now has significant contextuality to be meaningful: it is visible on the viewer's right. It is not enough to know that the pronoun *it* refers to the famous statue, or that the directional *right* is set in the context of New York City's geography. Why it is said at all is an essential part of its meaning—which is why the study of raw propositions continues to beguile so many epistemologists—and that is provided by the question "Where is the Statue of Liberty?" Truth is not restricted to the answer, but must include the question, since the question provides the scheme of coherence necessary for truth. If we assume that ordinary questioning consists in the projection of schemes of coherence; and if schemes of coherence are essential for understanding something as true; then truth cannot be found in any mere assertion of what is the case—such as found in ordinary declarative sentences. An ordinary question by itself is insufficient; but so is an ordinary answer by itself.

It may seem at first that the priority—in both senses—of questions is purely formal. Given any declarative sentence I can imagine a prior question that provides a certain contextuality or structure of coherence; but need I do this? Consider a simple declarative utterance: "The wine is on the table." By inversion we ask: "Is the wine on the table?" The point seems of gossamer significance. But we pause. We could also ask, "Where is the wine?" or "Is it on the table or the sideboard?" or "Is that the wine or the grape juice on the table?" or "Is the wine on or under the table?" Each of these questions asks in entirely different ways, from locating, to identifying, to precising, to intensifying. Yet each is answered by the same six words. But if there are variant and distinct prior questions, then the six-word answer is not the same in the case of locating or identifying. Surely the original declarative sentence does *not* mean the same in each case. So what the sentence "the wine is on the table," *means* is determined by what prior question is being asked or assumed. To locate and to identify are different acts, and in this case these differences depend not on the answer but on the question—or rather, the answers themselves differ because the questions differ.

Truth cannot therefore reside solely in the answer because what the answer means is in part determined by the prior question, either implicit or explicit. Questions therefore do not merely ask for the truth found in the answer; the scheme of coherence, which is the focus of ordinary questions, itself constitutes an original part of the truth. Reflection on our projection of possibility within the actual by means of schemes of coherence explains in part *how* we ask ordinary questions; but that truth matters responds to *why* we ask ordinary questions—which reinforces the earlier notion that asking rarely is reducible to single questions. What does it mean to say that "truth matters"? This cannot be translated into purely subjectivist emotion, as if some of us care about truth and others do not. The mattering of truth is not external to the phenomenon of asking (and hence thinking), but is an essential characteristic of it. Questioning makes truth matter; there is veridical anchorage in every asking. For asking makes no sense at all unless truth matters, just as promises make no sense to one lacking honor or integrity, nor does truth in a congenital liar. The truth that is necessarily assumed as a coherent condition for an asking may be as minimalist as wanting to know for the sake of our own advantage—What is the safest route out of this burning building?—but even in such selfish concern, truth matters, for we do not ask to be deceived, but to *know;* and whatever is known is true. Granted that what concerns me in the burning building is safety—one need not have any philosophical reverence for Truth with a capital *T* or even be honest in one's daily living, to have truth matter intensely in the context of learning the safest exit. Knowledge may be entirely utilitarian in such a case; but to ask which is the safest exit and where it is located, nevertheless is a request for truth. Such a question in such a situation does not ask for information or misinformation equally. We ask not for *an* answer but *the* answer; and thus asking is truth-directed and hence truth-entailing, to the extent that the asking enables a scheme of coherence. It is tempting but misleading to suggest that the asking provides the possible and the answer provides the actual; and only when possibility is linked to actuality is there truth. Attractive as such a suggestion may be, it loses much of its impact when we realize that *this* species of possibility is already *in* the actual, and this species of actuality is meaningful only in terms of its possibility.

In ordinary questions, the mattering of truth is contained in the concern for knowledge: I want to know the safest way out of the fiery building, and reflection shows that logically whatever is known is also true. In fundamental asking, truth itself, and not only knowledge of it, may matter independently. Yet even ordinary questioning may appreciate truth for its own sake, as when we delight in the refined asking that illuminates a truth in the study of science, art, or history. There is no need to begrudge respect for truth for its own sake even among the plainest folk engaged in the most banal endeavors. The point here is not philosophical elitism, but simply that even in the most pragmatic of situations, in asking for useful knowledge, the question as question necessarily seeks for genuine and not false answers, and thus truth matters whether we consciously "care about" it or not.

There is a bizarre challenge to this among certain counselors of the afflicted who adopt a radically nonveridical pragmatism in defense of certain therapies. What matters, they claim, is whatever eases distress. It is easy enough to believe that many people may be helped by accepting dubious or even obviously false doctrines. If believing in astrology or mystic forces of destiny helps a person overcome certain psychic fears or disorders, one may appreciate that the falseness of these doctrines does not gainsay their curative effects. Superstition may help some people overcome otherwise debilitating conditions, and it would be difficult to prohibit any techniques of misinformation that might alleviate terrible psychic pain. The "placebo effect" is, after all, well recognized. What astonishes, however, is some theorists' suggestion that the patient himself may realize such therapeutic cosmologies are false. Can a patient "believe" in what he knows to be false merely because such believing eases his mind? This, I have been assured by some, is entirely possible. I confess I do not know what *believe* means if I can believe what I *know* to be false; to believe means to hold as true or at least possibly true. A patient participating in a controlled experiment may realize that he may be given the placebo rather than the actual drug, yet this dubiety need not keep him from feeling better even if he unknowingly takes only the placebo. To *know*, however, that *only* placebos are given, and yet feel benefit, seems highly unlikely; but if we are to grant that these therapies do indeed work on occasion, it might seem that the traditional meanings of words like *belief* and *truth* must be reexamined.

This cost, however, is too steep. What seems far more likely is simply that the relation between therapist and patient has changed to the point where the latter has lost all sense of integrity, and has submitted, slavelike, to the therapist's manipulation. The cure may truly be far worse than the disease in such cases. Words as fundamental as *belief, knowledge, coherence,* and *truth* cannot be sacrificed on the altar of untroubled mindlessness. Truth matters even for the psychically haunted; indeed that there is truth rather than mere opinion may well be the only salvation. The syndrome of battered wives, for example, reinforces the reliability of truth: she does *not* deserve to be so treated; she should *not* be so pathetically grateful to his rare "kindnesses" that merely enslaves her more. In such cases, that there is truth rather than mere opinion can redeem.

These suggestions trouble in part because of the seeming analogue to fictive arts. Most lovers of drama do not believe in spriteful boys like Puck or Ariel nor in the magic of Oberon or Prospero, any more than opera patrons believe in Siegfried's magic sword or in the silly plots of some of the Italian bel canto marvels. Yet, during the performance perhaps we do accept magic provisionally; and if the production is truly fine, we may briefly find ourselves fearing the malicious wizardry of the Queen of the Night or elating in the powers of the magic flute. If we, in the audience, can truly fear, elate, worry about, get excited about, and even hope for, entirely imaginary and physically impossible things, then are we not to some extent "believing" them?—at least to the extent that patients may "believe" in therapies they "know" to be false? If art and therapy are analogous in this sense, we should perhaps adopt a more welcoming attitude toward the latter; but it is their disanalogy that indicts. The provisional acceptance of ghosts or magic in the arts is not inimical to truth for two reasons: first, we are asked to *pretend* that the magic is true; and second, there is a deeper respect for the truth inherent in the art that is not dependent on the literal acceptance of what is unbelievable. The patients enduring these weird therapies are not asked to pretend, but to accept as literally true what they know to be false; and their "acceptance" is a thwart to the integrity of truth itself. We may "suspend disbelief"—to use Wordsworth's felicitous phrase—without abandoning the trust *in* truth; but accepting as true what cannot be believed as a causal explanation of our real pain or trouble is injurious. We accept what the artist reveals about our emotions and feelings as true by deliberate bracketing of critical disbelief for the sake of letting this deeper truth emerge. There is no "deeper truth" in these bizarre therapies, there is only the narcotic of no longer caring. The therapy demotes our concern for truth through fantasy; the artist uses fantasy to enhance truth by playing. Figures of speech, such as hyperbole, are in the service of clarity, not obfuscation.

Were these distortions merely freakish incidents among the most unstable population, (meaning the therapists, not their patients or victims) they would scarce deserve mention. Unfortunately they proceed not only from unhealthy therapists but equally unhealthy educators; and the false piety of

relativism and nihilism has so pervaded our institutions of learning and popular entertainment that such pathetic submissions of integrity are now
endemic. We are told, for example, that we can *believe* in certain moral "systems," but that they cannot be true. What, then, does *belief* possibly mean?
It is not necessary to accept these radically nihilistic therapists, nor even their
sociological or educational partners, popular though they may be. Their
accounts are not genuine counter-evidence to this analysis; they are merely
sadly silly. We may lament their influence, but need not accept their critiques, nor their wanton abuses of language. Dictionaries have authority,
too. Ordinary asking is meaningful only because truth matters; even false
beliefs are held to be true, else they are not even beliefs.

It is not only the manner of asking, nor the topic, nor even the interrogative used that matters; it can also be the character of the asker himself.

"Is there any point to which you would wish to draw my attention?"
"To the curious incident of the dog in the night-time."
"The dog did nothing in the night time."
"That was the curious incident," remarked Sherlock Holmes.
  —"Silver Blaze," *The Memoirs of Sherlock Holmes*, A. C. Doyle.

Here the attention is drawn not to the logic but to the character of the
great sleuth. There seem to be certain people whose singular personalities
befit their raising certain kinds of questions. Doyle's skill in his depicting
Holmes gives a certain literary propriety to his asking that goes beyond mere
intelligence or forensic erudition; there is something about the man's
makeup, how he thinks, feels, judges, and responds to the natural and
human environments, that convinces us only Holmes could—or perhaps
should—ask quite like the way he does. Questions have questioners, and
who asks may be as relevant in understanding the mystery of asking as how
or what is asked, even in "ordinary" questioning. Any good detective, fic-
tional or actual, might observe that the dog, suspicious of strangers, did not
bark or attack on the night of the crime, thereby suggesting the perpetrator
was familiar with the dog, and thus narrow the list of possible suspects to a
very few. We as readers, however, take pleasure in the delightful way in which
Holmes leads us, adroitly and with a touch of condescension, to this realization. A commonplace point of investigative reasoning is here made dramatically poignant, so that it seems not common at all. It tells us far more
than who is guilty; it tells us about Holmes. But it also tells us about this
particular asking.

It may seem entirely counter-intuitive to suggest that who asks plays any role in the asking. Do claims depend on the claimant? "It is raining" surely informs us of the weather regardless of who asserts it.

Even as we consider this, though, we may hesitate. Coming from a professional weather forecaster, a congenital liar, a jokester, a poet, a pessimist setting out on his vacation, or an umbrella vendor may well make us hear the claim in varying degrees of reliability and meaning. Questions even more than claims may vary with the asker. It is sometimes difficult to discern when Socrates is asking literally or ironically, but he rarely, if ever, asks trivially; Polonius on the other hand, though fussy, rarely asks seriously; a grieving, anxious mother may ask "Where is he?" differently than the investigative police officer looking for the same boy. "Wherefore art thou Romeo?" possibly could only be asked by Juliet.

There is a general point noted here to the effect that all questioning presupposes a context, and who asks may constitute part of that contextuality. There is, however, a more significant point: the epistemological notions of subject and object are here inadequate. It is not the "subject" that asks but the person who asks; and this difference is weighty. For unlike "subjects," persons have character, and such character may play a determining role in the asking of a question. Just as propositionally similar sentences may mean different things given different questions that precede them, so propositionally similar questions may have different meanings depending on who asks them.

Technically, some epistemologists would argue that questions cannot be propositions because they do not assert what is the case; but there is no doubt that the propositional form, when inverted, becomes a question that seems to ask for a propositional response. Propositions are like paper currency that really does allow us to buy things and pay our debts, and hence has genuine value. But of themselves these notes are nothing; they achieve significance only when there is fiscal trust; the paper dollar works because of a general agreement by most of society to let it work, to accept it as reflecting a certain value *placed upon* it by established and ongoing convention. Without that convention and trust, the bill loses its purchase entirely and reverts back to mere paper. The proposition, unlike a spoken or written sentence, is sometimes thought as an abstract entity imbedded in sentences, and constituting the sole locus of truth. This makes truth itself an abstraction, conceived as a formal correspondence to what is the nonabstract actuality. As with the paper dollar, the proposition is an abstract convention with huge practicality, but no intrinsic truth or worth—just like the international dateline. Truth cannot reside in mere conventions or abstractions; and since questions contribute significantly to the meaning of claims, neither can they be accounted for merely by analysis of their proposition-like structure. Propositions, conceived in the context of contemporary analysis, do not rely on their speakers, as sentences do; and it is this nonreliance on the significance of the speaker that exposes their artificiality. Who speaks determines in part what spoken sentences mean, but propositions cannot; hence no proposition is ever adequate to the sentence. Who asks likewise determines the meanings of questions, and hence neither can questions ever be adequately represented in the propositional form alone. Just as the dollar must either represent specie, such as gold or silver, or an entirely imaginary standard of value, such as one-fifth of the minimum wage of a worker or the cost of a loaf of bread, so the propositional forms of questions must represent the entire asking procedure, which includes the questioner. Nor can the questioner be replaced by some imaginary propaedeutic state, such as "wanting to know," as if such "wanting" somehow avoids someone wanting.

This seems a mite troubling; for if every question presupposes a questioner, then every question seems unique, singular, and bereft of any universality; and if this is so it would seem to lose all possibility of philosophical authority. Questions would then seem nothing more than private, unshareable desires to know. This worry, however, is unfounded, since it is based on the false premise that universality is based entirely and exclusively on abstract formalism. The mother may ask where the boy is differently than the arresting narcotics officers, but since we have some sense of what it would mean to be a mother or an officer, the difference is not buried in radical egocentrism. Concrete universality is actually far more common and far less obscure than the abstract, though it may be considerably more difficult to account for by generalist governing rules. It is not necessary in this context to render such an account; it is enough to realize that the individual questioner can be a necessary part of questioning without losing the universality inherent in the coherence that is projected by the question. There is no reason to assume that lecturers in a classroom asking seemingly contentless questions are either paradigmatic of questioning or entirely lacking in contextual presuppositions amounting to content. "How high is Mount Everest?" may be asked by a teacher of geography in the Midwest plains of America, and the context of the classroom determines the kind of answer expected: so many feet or meters high. But a Tibetan climber is no less authentic in asking for the height of the highest in terms of days needed to scale it or even the spiritual powers of courage and fortitude required for the undertaking. If the

questioner is a schoolteacher asking about geography there is as much content as in the case of the Tibetan climber; formalism is itself a content.

This chapter is admittedly a detour of sorts; for it concerns not fundamental asking but simply how we ask ordinary questions and what must be
assumed in order to ask them. These reflections suggest the imagination is
able to project schemes of coherence that, when confronted *as* schemes of
coherence become questions. These question-originating projects provide
nonabstract possibility-within-the-actual, and in doing so establish connective links of coherence. Consistency is a purely analytic notion, keeping us
from contradicting ourselves. It cannot be both dark and light outside at the
same time, and so we distinguish—distinctions are always made to avoid
contradiction—between night and day. But to *connect* night and day requires
the projection of sequentiality, which then allows the succession from night
to day and from day to night to be used as temporal measuring. This connection is coherence, and not mere consistency. It can be further concretized
into a conventional system like a calendar. To focus on this ability as a form
of making-possible is to raise an ordinary question. This interrogative coherence is indeed presupposed by all claims that assert declarative sentences,
giving to the power to ask questions a certain rational priority. It is further
noted that each of the traditional interrogatives draws attention to specific
schemes of coherence. It is then suggested that in asking ordinary questions,
especially those that use traditional interrogatives, the goal is usable knowledge. The practical value of such knowledge does not prohibit us from
appreciating it for its own sake, however; and such appreciation turns our
consciousness from knowledge to truth. Whatever is known must be true,
and whatever is believed must be held as true, even if it be in fact false.
Questioning thus is possible only if truth can matter.

It is then suggested that not only do claims presuppose questions, but
that questioning itself is more than the mere propositional form affords,
for questioning is always contextually significant. Part of this context is who
asks and not merely what is asked or how it is asked. Subjects do not ask;
only persons ask; and only persons have character and judgment. These suggestions serve as a warning against minimalist reductionism—somehow
paring the act of questioning down to the skeletal edifices of pure formalism. Such paring is lethal—for skeletons lack both heart and brain; they
merely enclose or protect the organs of life—since questioning is possible
only for the living.

The realization of possibility as a species of enabling, discovered in earlier chapters, here becomes enormously helpful in understanding how we

ask ordinary questions. Mere abstract possibility need not provide more than mere skeletons, but enabling possibility—possibility within the actual—demands the kind of coherence only the living person can provide. Still, these reflections illuminate what we are designating as ordinary questioning. It is necessary to provide this sketch of how we ask ordinary questions in order to distinguish them from fundamental asking. But this is not all. Much of what we learn from this unpacking of the phenomenon of ordinary questioning also throws light on the extraordinary. We do not simply discard these lessons as mere counterfoils. This chapter may be a detour, but detours further the traveler along the route: this detour is an essential part of the asking mystery.

6

The Asker

The detour onto the common highway of raising ordinary questions should not distract from the journey up the rockier, rarer path of fundamental asking; for the detour itself reveals that who asks constitutes an essential part of questioning. It is thus possible now to ask, Who asks fundamentally? and by asking this we note the difference. Not all who can ask, do. Perhaps only a few can ask fundamentally, and this is troubling. In seeking to comprehend who asks, we must contrast with those who do not, the non-askers. What makes us ask is not merely our ignorance, but our abundance. Whoever lacks knowledge may be unaware of the lack, and thus does not ask at all. Neither do they ask who are sated with sufficient erudition, for there is nothing that compels them to probe deeply—they have no cause for asking. If our predetour reflections have any weight, we learn that the asker must be able to listen, and in suspenseful hearing to be surprised at his own existence. There is an adventure in asking that perhaps requires the courage-chafed warrior, struggling against not only external enemies but one's own frailty, fearing equally both defeat and trembling before it; yet, as adventurer, the asker seems blessed with a curious joy as well as a redeeming gratitude; for to ask is to acknowledge one's own non-necessity, and since one need not be, one is grateful to be at all. Yet, not altogether so; for at times the asker may prefer not to be, and deem one's own tenacious hold on life an unworthy fear, or dullest custom that has no service in it save to excuse a craven continuance. These dark ingratitudes may be essential to the asker's courage; they haunt without needing to eclipse; their endurance intensifies the asking.

Since who asks is an essential part of the asking it seems philosophically suggestive that fundamental asking must include our own existence within the world, bearing in mind the earlier caveat that no single question or topic—whether it be questioning God's existence, the nature of material objects, or even our own reflective agency—has priority. It is not *the one* question but the whole enterprise of asking itself that can be fundamental; and who asks is an essential part of it. Is it possible, then, to universalize this "who" without turning it into a purely formal subject? Can we, in other words, think about the asker with sufficient authority so as to avoid the twin perils of all self-reflection: either autobiographizing with merely personal and private sentiments, or formalizing into abstract and empty concepts? Success itself succeeds; great poets, sensitive religious teachers, rare philosophers, thinkers, artists, and historians of the highest rank have in fact managed this on the great occasions of cultural genius, and so *whether* it can be done need not afflict us with solipsistic paralysis. Who asks fundamentally? is thus a meaningful question; and the existence of paradigmatic successes offers the inquirer some purchase on what it means to ask in this way.

In the previous chapter, the reflections on ordinary questions reveal distinctions between the questioners and their dependence on truth. The victim within a burning building wants desperately to avoid a fiery death; when he asks for the safest exit, he does not ask for false and true answers equally; hence truth matters. But in this case, truth matters because of something else: his safety. Knowledge, which is truth-entailing, is here in service of practical concern. Yet ordinary people are not entirely without some sense of deeming knowledge and hence indirectly truth as having autonomous worth, as Aristotle wisely points out in the opening paragraph of the *Metaphysics:* we sometimes wish merely to satisfy our curiosity; we can actually take pleasure in the achievement of nonpractical knowledge for its own sake. It is this capacity for appreciating the intrinsic worth of knowledge that accounts for Aristotle's seemingly overly sanguine claim that it is in our nature to desire knowledge. Asking for the truth on behalf of some interest is thus distinct from asking for the truth merely because we want to know; but asking for truth for the sake of truth itself is distinct from both; and the three ways of asking reveal a hierarchy. Most everyday questions have practical significance, but some seek merely to satisfy curiosity or to please because it is delightful just to know things. It is imperative to resist identifying the latter as fundamental asking, which should be reserved only for seeking truth itself, not merely truth as a consequence of knowledge. Seeking truth itself requires a vivid sense of the asker, so that fundamental asking concretely confronts who asks in a way no other form of asking does. This does not mean that the topic must always be about oneself, as if "Who am I?" were the sole and supreme question; but it does mean that who we are as askers is revealed as critical to the coherence of the asking.

If the asker is to emerge, the spiritual character of the asker must manifest itself in specific ways. It is possible to suggest that, *as asker*, the image is more Dionysian than Olympian; more like David than Moses, more Greek than Roman; more Shakespeare than Dante; more Auden than Eliott; more Peter than Paul; more Lincoln than Washington; more Nietzsche than Hegel; more Socrates than Plato. Moses may be more important to the Hebrew religion than David; Washington, as inaugurator, more basic than Lincoln; Paul more orthodoxic than Peter; Hegel more rigorous than Nietzsche—but as askers the spirit is ranked otherwise. The Dionysian Socrates asks; the non-Dionysian Aristotle provides. These character comparisons cannot be taken too seriously. They are pointed out merely as a general sketch to catch a sense of the spirit behind asking. If pressed, they thwart their purpose. Aristotle and Hegel both ask fundamentally as well and Socrates sometimes answers.

The name *Socrates* on this list is helpful. He is an old man who loves young men, and bewildered by his passion, asks passionately about love, ping-ponging back and forth between moral restraint and shameless enjoyment of beauty. He fights bravely in battle, yet knows that fear is cautionary and wise, and audacity victorious and wise; and so he wonders how courage should be wise. He is pious; yet, charged with impiety for challenging the sacred, he confronts the torment of finding the holy an existential necessity for truth. In all these agonizing conflicts, he hesitates—though not as skeptic nor relativist, to select an opinion—somehow denuding fundamental truth by asking so fervently that truth becomes like an absent friend, or a lover who is briefly away, as is the boy in Shakespeare's sonnets. When truth, like the boy, is truly beloved, we say the lover knows him best; but when the beloved is absent, we still say the lover knows him best, but the absence throbs with an ache unimaginable, and from this ache we learn what love means. Do we really not know these things? Courage, love, wisdom, justice, piety, beauty—these are familiar. Unless we know them, and indeed know them well, they cannot be questioned. I know perfectly well what thirst is—you cannot tell me I do not "really" know thirst, nor can you succeed in showing me that thirst is "really" something else, like a stomachache or anger or cultural prejudice. Fear, like thirst, is not really something else—I know it immediately, without passwords—and fear confronted is courage-in-waiting. What unlocks the obvious to reveal the secret is asking—a pious, reverent, almost shamefully worshipful asking that alone unbuttons the shy modesty of truth for its own sake. So, I do know what thirst is, and what fear is, and knowing fear I am already knowing courage, even in lacking it. But though knowledge is always of the true, it is not clear that my knowledge of courage offers the truth of courage; for that step—the step from knowledge to truth—is enabled only by asking: the kind of asking Socrates does. What imperils here is the glib: How can this asking escape the ignominy of banal adages that comfort the sentimentally naive?

Gratefully, we know David and Socrates, Nietzsche and Auden are neither naive nor banal; and knowing they are not—just as we know thirst is not anger—we also know that fundamental asking is not glib. David, Socrates, Nietzsche, and Auden are not reducible to their claims—more than most of those whom we read with uneasy hope, they bare their skins; we know who they are beyond what they write. Each has a personality that emerges as palpably as their words exposing their flesh, exciting a species of trust, even in their vagaries. It is, after all, Meno who asks the great question whether virtue is teachable, Socrates who asks the dull, pedantic ones: first, What is the definition of virtue? and second, What is the definition of teaching? A thousand professors get this wrong: Meno's question is better than Socrates'; and in getting this wrong they miss entirely what is more significant: Socrates' asking is better—far better—than Meno's. Ten thousand professors get this wrong: depending on how we define *virtue* and *teaching*, the question whether virtue is teachable will follow. No. Only when we truly understand the cruel agony of teaching virtue do we know what teaching and virtue are. Socrates asks on this cruel, truth-revealing level; Meno cannot. Why don't good men always have good sons? This sounds like another question; but if we take it as part of Socrates' asking we hear the dramatic, bitter irony of some honest, virtuous man watching his own son rot into the malignancy of vice right before his eyes; and then the serpentine asking surprisingly bites the asker with toxic fangs: How can I be a good man since my son has grown so wicked?

To good men with bad sons this dread possibility cannot be entirely shunned. The guilt police may well rush in to arrest any feelings of responsibility, enforcing the opiate of all conscience by cheating him of fault; but the father knows too well. Why be a father unless moral educating is possible? If moral training is impossible, why do we care about what is being taught our children at all? Fathers—and states as well—would then not matter. There is so much evidence the curers of grief seem to overlook. Children can be taught to respect others, to have good manners, to speak politely, to esteem themselves, to accept responsibility. They can also be taught to disregard others, to satisfy all urges, and even to develop unholy urges they otherwise might not have, to cheat, to profane language, and to deceive. Those taught the virtues live much more nobly than those taught the vices, especially the vulgarities. Fathers know this. To see their sons become wretched through vice therefore seems a blight on their own success as teachers. The bad son of a good father scalds fiercely and ironically, and the misread *Meno* offers this painful truth to the unhearing who note it not at all. What, the professors say, does this dramatic element, if present, offer to the formal argument? We want reasons, not passions. Perhaps a distraught father might agonize over a wayward son, but what has this to do with a work in philosophy? Do not ask who Socrates is, or even who Meno is; we care only about the validity of their arguments.

Purely formal validity is never the central point in fundamental asking; it is not the point in Plato's aporetic dialogues, either; despite the Cambridge epistemologists. Good thinkers care about validity, to be sure; but that is not the only or even dominant concern in fundamental asking. The drama is essential precisely because character is the soul of drama; the haunted father of a wanton son is not a puzzle to be solved or even a problem to be addressed; he is a surprise. His wonder, too, surprises: perhaps, just because he has a bad son he dare not think himself a good father. Letting his son become a man, of course, frees the youth, making him at first partly, and then perhaps fully, responsible for what he becomes. The father knows this as well; but fathers do influence and prepare the son's character to accept this responsibility, and we, who observe the unfolding of the drama, see the chasm widen before us. Meno's excellent question has been adroitly subsumed into the cruelty of Socratic asking. No mere formal validity suffices now. What emerges is the character of the asker. Socrates—and not merely Socrates' arguments—alone can confront the gaping abyss. Who he is becomes a part of his argument. Since the development of character is part of what is meant by moral education, as well as the craft of dramatists, why should this surprise us? It is not the "real" Socrates, living in Athens, but the dramatized Socrates living in the dialogues whose character becomes essential for asking. We must never forget that the stunning first line of the dialogue, in which Meno raises the question about virtue being teachable, initiates the five-dialogue confrontation with this asking; and it is precisely when the question ceases to be Meno's and becomes Socrates' that its dreadful truth emerges. For Socrates is indicted precisely because Athens believes that virtue, and its opposite, vice, are indeed teachable; and Socrates defends his activities by revealing his character as one who has not brought harm—vice—to the youth of Athens; implying that he, too, accepts the principle behind the indictment. Not only must virtue be teachable, but character matters in the teaching; for Socrates does not, in the *Apology*, defend his *views*, but defends himself.

If virtue can be taught, it can also be learned; and herein lies the suffering: it can, but need not, be learned. The son who learns virtue from his father emerges as an autonomous, worthy agent; so does his brother who does not learn virtue, but turns away. We must ask not only what it means for virtue to be taught but also what it means for it to be learned, and with this realization, who learns becomes not a mere tissue of necessary and sufficient conditions but an essential, nonreducible element in our confronting Meno's question with Socratic asking. Who teaches and who learns are no less troubling than who asks, for it inserts into our asking about learning nonreducible elements—unique persons—who cannot in principle be accounted solely by reference to their origin or by the roles they play in any grander scheme whatsoever. The use of the concrete image of fathers educating sons, however, gives us a resource not entirely unworthy of further reflection. There is a paradox in the education of our children: since they are ours we are obliged to pass on to them the sacred inheritance of our cultural worth; but since this educating is devised to let them become adults, we seek to make them independent. Every parent knows this curious, painful, joyous dilemma: the greatest act of love may well be letting go. Like death, the empty nest is inevitable; and since billions of people go through this every generation, it is obviously not an impediment to success. The ubiquity, however, is no solace to the ache; what may fluster us is that it seems a necessary pain, perhaps even a welcome pain—would we prefer *not* to suffer it?

To speak of good fathers with bad sons requires the focus on unique persons, thereby showing that who teaches, learns, and asks, is essential. Not only does every statement presuppose a question for its coherence, every question demands a unique, nonreducible person as asker. Since the character of this asker is not uncommunicable—for that is precisely what drama makes available—we are not left with radical subjectivism or relativism; indeed the appreciation of character, and hence of "who," may be more communicable, and hence more "universal," than abstract considerations of necessary and sufficient conditions. Dramatic presentation and development of character succeed in part because we as audience or readers are, after all, also unique persons. We are more than our species and certainly more than our origins; so whoever considers only species must be thwarted in the attempt to understand who we are. Since great drama reveals more than merely the species, even as it accomplishes universality—for we are not all Hamlets but Hamlet is nevertheless a universally available resource for learning who we are—it seems that the concrete can be at the same time the universal. In the second chapter it was noted that possibility-within-the-actual is enabling, and thus lies at the basis of asking. We now note that universality (necessity)-within-the-actual enables learning as asking. Reflection on this suggestive modality must be delayed until subsequent chapters. For now the focus is still on the asker.

The anecdotal reading of Socrates struggling with moral education is a helpful propaedeutic. We must now focus more specifically on why the asker—who asks?—is essential for fundamental asking. Unless the asker matters it were impossible for asking to be about ourselves; we could not ask who we are nor consider any other asking that contains our own existence as integral to it. When David considers the heavens he is led to ask about himself; and even though he formulates his wonder in terms of "man," the unique, nontransferable person we learn to know from our cultural resources as David, matters for the asking. The paradox is that only the unique David can ask as he does; but that we can hear him ask, take surprise in what we hear, and thereby become askers ourselves, not unlike the lodestone metaphor in Plato's *Ion*, showing how the magnetism of the original genius (Homer) passes though and communicates to the iron pieces (the rhapsode and then the audience) that link themselves to the chain.

The importance of the nonreducible asker has vast significance. One thing is obvious: if I ask how I fit into the world, whatever the world is must be able to accommodate and account for my asking; otherwise I would have to ask not only how I fit into the world, but how I do *not* fit into the world, since asking about the world would then put me beyond it or outside it. Unfortunately we sometimes use the term *world* to designate the totality of nonpersonal objects, which then forces us to ask either how we fit into a world inadequate to persons, or how we ourselves become nonselves in fitting into such a world. Such usage is perilous in the extreme, for it has seductive allure. There seems to be a vast authority to the world, the anchor to all asking, the ground of all answers. The world outranks us both in importance and reality. It pre-exists us and outlasts us and must somehow be the origin of who and what we are. Yet, it is also our dwelling, our object, the mute bearer of our abuses, the stage for our drama. For some, *world* equates with *reality*, which would mean it is the ground of truth itself—even truth about persons. These ambiguities can, of course, be tagged, defanging some of the threat, but even with refining labels the peril persists, for the contrast between reflective, autonomous beings and the rest of the universe is too deep to be sidelined merely with precising adjectives.

To ask how I fit into the grand scheme puts me beyond the scheme, for no scheme as scheme is adequate to such reflective asking. To ask how I fit into the world is merely to treat the world as a scheme, which belies what the world is; but to ask how I belong in the world treats both world and asker as transchematic, i.e., real. Schemes provide for ordinary questions by the enabling possibility that grounds coherence, or by purely abstract projections that provide conventions; but fundamental asking must seek enabling not in schemes but in reality, which is always and necessarily the world containing the asking dweller. To insist on the primary givenness of the asking person creates an entirely artificial sense of a denuded "I" such as beguiles both Descartes and Fichte, in which a real person becomes an abstract scheme called a subject. To rank the world as other and independent of the asker creates an entirely artificial sense of a mysterious, external entity or thing-in-itself such as beguiles Locke and the misreaders of Kant, in which the meaningful world becomes an abstract scheme called an object. The very word *fit* suggests a purely schematic coherence, as 3:00 P.M. "fits" into the scheme of clocked time, and thus has no meaning at all outside that scheme. Our real dwelling in the real world is entirely abused by the impropriety of raising ordinary questions to achieve fundamental asking. Once we lose sight of David and Auden, Nietzsche and Socrates, as unique persons, asking because of and about their nonschematic existence, both world and self will ever be unavailable, and questioning will be restricted to fitting tokens within abstract schemes of coherence.

The paradox in fundamental asking is this: to arrive at the real world rather than a merely schematic "world," it is necessary to ask about the asker, which seems to focus not on the world, but only on a privileged but very tiny part of it. This paradox, like most true, philosophical paradoxes, is not a misological block to inquiry, but when embraced, offers the kind of rare insight into truth that redeems all the efforts, frustrations, and provisional silliness we as thinkers must endure in order to rejoice so profoundly at discovery. Kant claims that only two reflections fill him with awe: the starry heavens above him and the moral law within him. What he does not specifically say—though perhaps, as the supreme synthesizer, he should—is that we cannot have the one without the other. For it is only because of my own unique moral integrity that the starry heavens can amaze; and it is only because of a vastness that outreaches my grasp that this moral integrity—the uniqueness of my "soul"—becomes awesome. Before these two sublime reflections, since both exceed my grasp, I can but ask. Yet, this asking is not merely an indication of ignorance, but of joyous or at least awe-inspiring wonder which itself is veridical: there is *truth* and not merely truth-seeking in the wonder. David's psalm reveals this as well: the asking reveals not merely the firmament nor even what man is, but why we should matter so much more than the firmament. Who are we, tiny specks of dust that, in range and scope far outranked by the vastness of the universe, matter more than what contains and surrounds us? Such confrontations are fundamental because they unite the asker with the world. We are not just "in" the world, along with shells, gravel and moons, but dwell in it; and the world is not just the place where all this happens, like some vast attic containing out-of-place, discarded lamps, broken tricycles, and Christmas ornaments in July, but the anchor to our asking and the home to our dwelling. World is not external, nor is the unique person who asks a mere item located in an indifferently vast dustbin; nor is the asker merely "internal." Our being in the world changes what the world is, and the world, as dwelling-place, changes who we are.

It is both possible and advantageous to ask about things and events in the world as mere objects, available for our perception; it is even legitimate to ask about the "external world" as an object—the object that contains all other objects—as long as we recognize that such questioning is but ordinary questioning without any credentials for fundamental asking. In asking about entities in the world, or the external world itself as a vast container, the term *world* is used as a scheme of coherence; but in fundamental asking about our being in the world and the world being our dwelling, the world is real. Since all asking, whether fundamental or ordinary, confronts projective possibility and hence coherence, the reality of the asker must emerge in fundamental asking, since this asker is part of the coherence. This does not imply we must know the name of the asker, or even that we know many things about the asker from other, nonasking, resources. Reference to recognized askers such as Socrates and David merely exemplifies the importance of the character. Even if we did not know the name of the author of the psalms, the kind of asking contained in them tells us something about who asks them, though not as much as we do know about him from texts and sculpture. Knowing more about David teaches us more about his asking than if we were not to know about him.

The essential integration of the asker with the world may seem sufficiently nontraditional so as to provoke no little critical dubiety: surely, we might suggest, the world is the world just because it is not dependent on our asking; and our character, being unique, as individuals must stand out from the world. The response to this criticism is guarded: the world is indeed separable from the asker in the mode of ordinary questioning in which the world is naught but a scheme of coherence; and asking characters, when using schemes of coherence, do indeed stand out from it. It is only when both asker and world are not seen as schemes but as reality that fundamental asking requires their intimate integration. On this level, both asker and world become coherent reality—that is, reality that is in its essence enabling of coherence. The world coheres; the asker coheres; and asking integrates world and asker, becoming the ultimate coherence. It is precisely because the asker is a character and not a mere formal subject, that in asking about oneself, the real (nonschematic) world is also asked; and in asking about the real world the real asker is also asked. The specific question is therefore of secondary, though by no means insignificant, importance; for questions about the world, if asked fundamentally, will reveal the questioner, and questions about the questioner will reveal the world. There are, outside of imagined schemes, only two synthesizing realities—beings that themselves, in their essence or nature, provide coherence: the world as asked and the asker in the world. When these real beings themselves cohere together, fundamental asking takes place.

All authentic asking entails some sense of answering, but isolating the specific answer—achieving knowledge—depends on this asking, and is not necessary in order for the asking to be legitimate. The nature or essence of the specific asker need not be identified, but the asking reveals the uniqueness of the asker even if vaguely. David's joyous awe at the significance of man in the universe is part of his glorious asking; and if we listeners are entirely lacking in this awe, we cannot hear or participate in the asking, though we may recognize the question in its abstraction, and thereby run the grave risk of thinking in terms of ordinary questions. It is the reality of both asker and world that is lost if the uniqueness of the asker is not included, and this loss is almost inevitable if we focus merely on the question as question. The phenomenon of philosophical inquiry provides us with a special instance in which this kind of asking occurs.

7

Inquiry

Philosophical inquiry is the paradigm of fundamental asking, and our intellectual history is fortunately provided with a small but meaningful number of great inquirers. The presence in our libraries of thinkers such as Plato, Kant, Aristotle, Nietzsche, and Heidegger assures us that inquiry can and does occasionally reach the highest rank, and consequently reflection on the nature of inquiry is not purely speculative. We have available actual, readable successes: they are works worth reading, and not merely because of their historical, but because of their veridical, importance. Yet even to recognize these masterpieces of philosophical inquiry is already troubling, for we may well admit their rank and yet still be critical of them. We may read them and disagree as to their proper interpretation, or read them and reject their analyses, or even read them as distorting the truth and leading us astray in profound ways; and yet they remain as paradigms of philosophical inquiry. Nevertheless, they do exist; and they have deserved status as exemplars of critical and speculative reasoning; and because they are indeed on our shelves we can point to them or refer to them and be thereby assured that inquiry is not a mere abstract possibility or ideal, but is actual. This may seem a minimalist point to some, but its importance cannot be dimmed, for the simple modal logic cannot be avoided; whatever is actual is also possible. Our concern here, however, is not with their actual existence, but with the possibility within their actuality: what enables them to be.

As inquiry is essentially a mode of asking, what in part enables philosophical inquiry are the paradoxes inherent in it—and attention is directed to the plural. There is more than one paradox. Plato's *Meno* gives us but one; and in presenting it as a paradox it is entirely misread if we find the dialogue providing an answer. If I don't know what I'm looking for I can't look and if I do know, I have no need to look. Paradox. In fact, however, I both know and do not know, hence I can inquire or look. Paradox solved. No, the paradox just is that I can be both knowing and unknowing of the same thing at the same time. The paradox persists, but no longer as an impediment to thought but as a resource for thinking, for only if we are both wise and ignorant about what matters most can we ask fundamentally at all. If a paradox is solved it was never a paradox in the first place; it was merely a problem, usually resting on a misunderstanding of what certain terms mean, so that when the terms are clarified the bewilderment ceases. Such analyses matter because they save us from contradiction; they do not resolve paradoxes. The wise realize that philosophical inquiry as a species of fundamental asking is truly paradoxical in at least four ways, none of which can be rendered unbewildering merely by refining terms—noble as such propaedeutics may be.

The four paradoxes just mentioned are rooted in four essential characteristics we normally assign to philosophical inquiry: (1) it must seek truth, and indeed truth for its own sake; (2) it must be a species of reasoning, and indeed a reasoning that reflects the nature and meaning of reason itself; (3) it must be rooted in a knowledge that is also a kind of ignorance, indeed a kind of knowledge that knows its own ignorance; and (4) both the asker and the asking must belong significantly to the asked-about. Each of these four characteristics, that de facto seem to be recognized as belonging to actual inquiry, contains a deep and troubling paradox. Perhaps much will be gained if we understand these are not simply conceptual anomalies; they are also wondrous ironies. Here the term *irony* is not the Swift-like assertion that intends the opposite of what is literally said, as when Antony refers to Caesar's assassins as *honorable* as he shows the crowd their dishonor; rather it is the more painful sense in which an ardent advocate brings about the opposite and often cruel result, as when we say it is sadly ironic that pacifism often helps bring about a war, or that the sincerely dispassionate Angelo in *Measure for Measure* should succumb so passionately to Isabelle's icy beauty. Perhaps among the cruelest of such ironies are those akin to

Beethoven's deafness: the creator of such glorious music, most deserving to hear it, cannot. (It is disturbing that famed literary handbooks tend to speak only of Swiftian irony, and not of the peculiarly dramatic sense of irony that is far more effective when used well.) Such irony also has its comic side, particularly when a singularly fitting sense of justice is satisfied, as when Angelo at the end of the play is trapped by his own cunning. To suggest there is irony in the four paradoxes of inquiry is not a mere literary veneer; it dares to alter fundamentally our comprehension of paradox, giving it a surprising, existential, and even dramatic meaning that has both tragic and comic elements. Fundamental asking may be essentially, at its roots, dramatically ironic. A sketch of these ironic paradoxes may be helpful.

1. It is glib enough to say that truth should be sought for its own sake. What, though, can this possibly mean? When we say, for example, that pleasure can be enjoyed just for its own sake we mean there is no further need to justify it. Why have pleasure? Because it pleases. I do not need to add that *if* I have pleasure there will be further benefits resulting from it, though this may be true. Perhaps if I enjoy pleasure I will also, as a result, be less irksome to my friends. But I do not need to have such consequences to make sense of my pleasure—pleasure is self-justifying. Can we really say that truth is like pleasure? Contemplating truth may bring us pleasure, to be sure, but then we seek truth for the sake of pleasure rather than for the sake of truth. This is not yet a paradox, and certainly it is not yet an irony; it is merely a challenge. Suppose, though, we accept the claim that truth is self-justifying. In the case of pleasure we mean there is no need for further justification. Is truth, then, like an answer? Is it the final resting place for the asker? Curiosity can be satisfied by the achievement of knowledge, and since knowledge must be true it seems truth can be similarly justified—as a species of satisfaction. But truth is a necessary condition for knowledge, it is not equated with it. It may be possible to justify knowledge on the basis of satisfying curiosity, but do we say this of truth? According to the myths of the late eighteenth century, Lessing was offered two options by God: in his right hand was truth, in his left was the search for truth. Lessing, after reflecting, chose the left, leaving truth itself to God. We accept this as a nice story. But how can I choose to search for truth unless I want truth itself? Is not Lessing being supremely false to his putative love for truth if he turns down the one guaranteed access to it? This is loving untruth, not truth. We begin to sense dramatic irony here. The most deserving of truth, Lessing, in the end, turns away from it. It also sounds like a paradox. One of the most severe indictments we can bring against anyone is the confusion of ends and means, or

justifying the latter on the basis on the former. We praise the warrior who builds an army necessary to defend our nation; but when the war is won, we censure the same warrior for continuing to fight just because he has grown fond of it. If the love of truth is ranked above truth, have we not ranked the means above the end? If truth is ranked above the love for it, then is not philosophy mad in ranking its own endeavor as intrinsically worthwhile? This is but a sketch. We begin to see the ironic paradox; for the moment that suffices.

2. Philosophical inquiry, as fundamental asking, is a species of reasoning. What does this mean? It is entirely unlike reason in any other sense: it does not follow rules inevitably, and draw conclusions by way of inference, as deduction does; nor does it gather support for generalities as induction does. It does not break down complexities into simples as analysis does. It does not test hypotheses as science does, nor does it classify as taxonomy does; nor does it speculate about motives as jurists do, nor figure out what happened as detectives do, nor poll the populace as pollsters do; nor does it solve equations as mathematics does, nor ease our living as technology does, nor guide our conduct as morality does. All these are ways of being reasonable, and philosophers certainly do reason in these ways as *part* of their inquiry, but inquiry as inquiry, does not do any of these things. Yet Plato, Kant, Nietzsche, Aristotle, Heidegger, and Augustine do inquire, and we think of them as reasoning when they do. We might suggest that all these other uses of reason are designed to achieve answers to specific questions, whereas philosophical reasoning as inquiry seeks not to give answers but to deepen questions. To "deepen questions" however seems to make things muddier than clearer. There is a touch of paradox already in this: Why should I, as reasoner, seek to be more, rather than less, confused? This hint of paradox becomes ironic when philosophical asking seems to produce misology, as is noted in Plato's *Phaedo* and in the Dialectic of Kant's *Critique of Pure Reason*. The more we think, and the more we become fascinated with asking, the greater the dangers of skepticism, relativism, and nihilism emerge. Ordinary, decent, intelligent folk are rarely inclined to any of these three hideous dispositions of reason-hating, unless provoked by dangerous philosophers. It seems that it becomes unreasonable to be reasonable, precisely when reason itself is pressed too hard.

That philosophical inquiry may lead to the misologies in skepticism, relativism, and nihilism may seem almost a tragic irony; but there is a comic irony in the scramble of philosophical theorists to define—or even to understand—what reason itself is. We say, in all seriousness—or is it the comic

bubble of pomposity waiting to be pricked by a child's mischievous pin?—
that we are reasoning about what reason is. How can I know I am being reasonable in my quest if the nature of reason is the object of my quest? If
anyone other than a philosopher were to admit to such folly, they would be
accused of begging the question. Is not all serious inquiry at bottom a species
of question-begging, and hence not serious but playful—a comic folly? The
ironies run deep in this shallow stream. To be sure, the tragic irony of philosophic misology may be more threatening, making us possibly guilty; but
the comic irony of seriously playing denudes us in our folly, enabling not
guilt but shame. A deeper analysis of how asking is a species of reasoning
can be found in chapter 9.

3. We are more familiar with the third irony—that ignorance is a way
of knowing—but it is this very familiarity that tends to darken, as clouds
darken the day, the true paradox inherent in this ironic wisdom. The problem first needs to be precisely stated. There is neither paradox nor irony in
knowing one thing and not knowing another, as I know that Chicago is
north of New Orleans but do not know the ingredients in a chef's famous
sauce. It is troubling only when my knowledge seems to require a kind of
ignorance, or my ignorance a kind of knowledge, as when not knowing the
outcome of the day's battle is essential for the self-knowledge that is courage:
I cannot know in advance the limits of my courage if I am to be courageous;
but courage is a species of self-knowledge painfully wrought by this very
ignorance. It seems then that in order to know myself I must be ignorant of
myself. This is a paradox. There is also irony here: the one tormented by his
own dubiety about his courage, facing his cowardice, is more profoundly
courageous than one certain of his courage, and who, though quite capable
of great daring in facing dangers may pale before the dread need to face his
own vulnerability. It is not merely courage that is ironically paradoxical, but
it is enough for the sake of the preliminary sketch to recognize that courage
is a species of self-knowledge and that I cannot know in advance the limits
of my courage. This is why we pray for courage, which itself requires courage.

4. To state the fourth paradox is the only easy thing about it. The subject knows; the object is known; how can the subject-knower become the
object-known without losing its autonomous status? To say I am both subject and object does not solve the dilemma, it merely restates it. To argue
that self-reflection is a fact does not help either. We know it is a fact. We
want to know how it is possible and what it means, for there is a vivid sense
in which I never can be merely an object. In this way is the paradox of self-
inquiry often raised. The irony is that in seeking to explain how knowledge

of oneself is possible, the true, deeper problem is overlooked: it is not how I know myself that troubles, it is how I do not know myself. It is self-ignorance that stuns us, not self-knowledge—although self-knowledge in its deeper sense requires a grasp of what it means to be ignorant of oneself. Is not Descartes right in at least this, that the *cogito* is certain; I not only know for certain I exist, I also know *what* I am—a thinking being? How then is it possible to be ignorant about who and what I am? Even as we suggest this to ourselves, however, it is obvious that we are yet mysterious to ourselves, even in ordinary, everyday instances—as when we are dubious about our motives, unsure of how we will react to forthcoming events, or muddled about our feelings. Is there a greater irony than this, that in seeking to respond to philosophy's god-father, the Delphic injunction to know thyself, we forget to ask how we can even *be* ignorant of ourselves? If philosophical inquiry is indeed the paradigm of fundamental asking, and if both self and world provide coherence not as schemes but as reality, then our being mysterious to ourselves is itself a mystery, indeed an ironic mystery.

These four ironies are by no means unexpected. Even ordinary people realize that philosophers are concerned with the great questions—and not the great answers—though they may not see the irony in this. They also recognize philosophers use reason and argumentation, and must somehow reflect on reasoning itself. Since most people are vaguely aware that inquiry assumes a kind of ignorance, neither are they surprised that philosophers should embrace their ignorance. Of the four paradoxes, seeking truth for its own sake may be the most bewildering to the ordinary thinker; but since the intrinsic worth of truth is also the most bewildering for the philosopher himself, this irony is not remarkable. What though, does all this mean? If philosophical inquiry is fundamentally ironic, what does this tell us?

Originally, irony is a figure of speech, like metaphor or metanomy. In classical literature the purpose of a figure is not embellishment but clarity, especially clarity conceived as intensifier. When Hotspur, "from this nettle, danger . . . pluck(s) the flower, safety," we hear, not merely a prettiness of metaphoric figure, but an insight: courage alone finds true safety only in outfacing danger. Irony, as a figure, intensifies, by showing that asking finds in the coherence of things a curious "fitness" that can be either cruel or comic. Both cruelty and comedy intensify our alertness to the very unexpected fitness that itself provides a species of coherence. When the warrior's trust in the institution of the army beguiles Othello into cruel distrust in the counter-institution of marriage, we see a fitness in the presentation: it makes the raveling of plot connected to the unraveling of character. There is a

strange acquiescence, as if we were nodding to ourselves, saying: it is fitting—dramatically coherent—that a warrior, whose strength lies in the trust
of his officers, reveals his weakness in the unfair mistrust of his wife. It is
through this irony that the mere sequence of plotted events that make up
the story is given an added aesthetic coherence to the art form, thereby giving to the drama a unity it otherwise would lack. One way we discover or
achieve coherence is noting similarities, and if the element that constitutes
Othello's greatness is isomorphic with the element of his collapse, we then
connect, by the coherence of the ironic figure, the great with the tragic,
intensifying the meaning, truth, and enjoyment of the play.

Irony as a literary figure however is a contrivance. It is controlled by the
master craftsman, one of many tools used to make his work a single or unified accomplishment. How are we to understand an artistic contrivance as
fitting the search for truth? The essence of irony, both literary and real, lies
in a coherence achieved by turning back on itself, in a way that mocks banality. By its focus on the peculiarly, or even macabre, "fitting," we see it as a
species of reflexive reasoning. It achieves unity, hence it is a form of reasoning; but it always achieves this unity by turning back on itself, hence, reflexive. Since asking provides coherence, ironic asking turns back on itself by
mocking itself, thereby providing an unexpected, perhaps deeper, and perhaps surprising, coherence. The questioner is stunned by the illumination
provided by his own questioning rather than, as expected, by the muting
answer.

There need be no irony at all in a philosopher's answering synthesis. We
do not need to wait to see what the asking discovers, for this point must be
emphasized: the irony and the paradox are in the very reflexive coherence
provided by the asking, not in the answering. There may be further irony in
some answers, but that is irrelevant here. The key to the irony of inquiry lies
in its reflective as well as its reflexive nature. These terms, reflective and
reflexive, are discussed in greater detail in chapter 9. We who are able to see
and hence represent all things else, cannot, save in mirrored imagery, represent ourselves. When we ask fundamentally, we find ourselves cast adrift
from the moorings of ordinary reasonings—schemed questioning that provides coherence to discoverable and, in principle, testable answers—and
forced to confront what is most meaningful to us: our own unique personality and consciousness, which evade us as soon as the traditional canons of
access and critique are put into place. The mockery of "Physician, heal thyself!" looms as inevitable. Yet, this very mystery of our ownmost intimacy is
perforce illumined by irony, as Beethoven's deafness curiously illuminates

his music just by the irony of the worthiest ear in history barred from the worthiest music. By reflecting on his deafness we recognize how precious our hearing of his music is. Some lovers of music even suggest his deafness gave greater majesty to his later works, as Demosthenes' speech impediment forced him to greater oratory. That we are mysterious to ourselves forces us to find a greater resource to truth in our asking than in reticent answers.

This reflection on irony cannot be glib. Give the banner of "Socratic irony" to the banal, and the results are obscene. Whatever they do not want Socrates to say, they label *ironic*, defanging all that bites and stings. Since the banal are banal just because they cannot conceive of anything worthwhile lurking outside the comfort of received wisdom, and recognizing that Socrates is a revered figure, the weapon of the label *irony* is used as the great equalizer, grinding the tough meat of true inquiry into the palatable pabulum of the toothless. Socrates is not "ironic"—that is, sarcastic—when he calls Euthydemus and his dazzling brother impressive and fascinating. He is genuinely dazzled by them. If there is irony here, it is because the sophistic brothers sound so much like himself, and he must learn through a highly developed sense of comedy why he is not like them. There is irony in the *Charmides* when the virtue of *sophrosune*—self-control—is accompanied by Socrates' seeming lack of it when he espies the youthful beauty winking through the boy's open robe. The irony is intensified when we realize that unless Socrates does love the boy, the dialogue would not take place at all. That the paradoxes of fundamental asking are ironic does not give license to amused assurance; rather it warns us that what is at stake is truth itself. *At stake* here means in danger. Not only is the danger that of banality, in which irony is a license for anesthesia; but danger in the sense that, recognizing the difficulty inherent in the paradox of remaining mysterious to ourselves, we take this as an excuse to abandon inquiry altogether, except as a species of parlor games for the amused intellectual who finds philosophy just fun—as Euthydemus does.

Irony, however, is not merely a conceptual self-reflecting; it is also a feeling, the central components of which are the dread and surprise at being a plaything of ungoverned fate, distantly amused at its producing these curious parallels of meaning. Beethoven's deafness was not the result of his own planning, or any other human planning as far as we know. Apparently modern physicians could have cured it, a fact that somehow seems to make it worse. The deafness undoubtedly had a natural, identifiable cause, so we are not assuming a malicious spirit arranging it merely to excite our appreciation of cruel symmetry. Yet, even as we accept a species of unsavory coincidence as the causal factor, we cannot escape the existential irony read off this troubling history. Why him of all people? We shrug. Sometimes, we say vacuously, we are the victims of an ironic twist of fate. But this shrug is voluptuous insouciance: how can we shrug off something as epistemically muscular as this? The cause of Beethoven's deafness may be coincidental to his genius, but what it means for there to be the "Ode to Joy" unheard by its creator is not shruggable. Irony here is palpably confronted and thus felt. It is seemingly unseemly for philosophy to take the passions seriously, at least in an age when reason is conceived formally and hence without content. The truth-seeker, as inquirer, however, cannot fall into this misological trap. Irony hurts; comedy is fundamentally cruel, though its cruelty can be softened by warm, amused affection. Since self-inquiry is not the same as a mere taxonomy of formal inferences, we must credit both the passions and the curious measure we take of our vulnerability to the arbitrary powers of fortuity.

Is irony, as felt, merely our ignorance; is it merely a different way of seeing our finitude? Even if we accept this suggestion provisionally, we still cannot dismiss it with a shrug. Irony is not the same as *being* ignorant, though it may be a way of thoughtful confrontation *of* our ignorance—that is, it is a way of thinking and feeling about our being ignorant. To be able to think existentially about our finitude—ignorance—is, however, to triumph over it in some respect, since this makes our very ignorance, when confronted, a resource of our own meaning, and hence is a *thoughtful* ignorance, which is as paradoxical and ironic as we can get. Thoughtful ignorance? Is this an oxymoron? An oxymoron is itself a figure of speech—it is not a mere inconsistency or self-contradiction, although popular discourse has abused its meaning recently. Jocularly to suggest that "army intelligence" is oxymoronic misuses the term; I use the term here properly: as a figure, and hence, as a clarifier or intensifier. A wet dryness is not an oxymoron because it does not reveal anything, but fiery ice is a legitimate oxymoron because it does reveal the power of ice to hurt as if it were burning. Thoughtful ignorance may seem at first a mere inconsistency, but when seen as an oxymoronic figure we recognize that philosophical inquiry depends in part on our own awareness of what it means to be ignorant—and also what it means to be vulnerable to the ironies of fate. To call them ironies of fate is not to attribute causal power to some mysterious, spiritual marionetteer, but neither does it dismiss them as mere figments of a literary imagination. These ironies hurt, and the hurt is real. These ironies roil our reason, and the ensuing confusion is real; but these ironies also illuminate, and the learning that comes from them is true; and being true is grounded in what is real. The reasoning that is roiled by irony is but a species of reasoning, for inquiry itself is also reasoning, and contains necessarily the paradoxical and ironic as distinguishing characteristics.

The very fact we can distinguish various ways of reasoning shows us that reason is able to reflect on itself. This is what gives philosophical inquiry its peculiar rank; but is there irony in this? The merely ignorant do not inquire; the knowingly ignorant inquires in part because he wants to know what he now knows he does not know, and knows enough to be able to formulate his asking in a proper way. What is more often overlooked is that being knowingly ignorant is not enough for inquiry; we must also be aware of the worthiness of the questioning. There is sad pathos in seeing a fine mind wasting its energies on trivialities, as the image of the great Napolean Bonaparte ruling sadly over his little island of St. Helen's evokes a sense of waste, however deserved. It may have been nobler to have executed him. To accept the judgment that philosophers ask rather than merely answer the great questions leaves unasked the origin of the adjective. How do we judge what is great and what is trivial? If by *great* here is meant at least "worthy of being questioned," we can see that the reflective nature of philosophical inquiry must include the power to assess worth. We are aware of the worthiness of the great questions because they are about ourselves, raised in a manner such that the very *way* we ask is intended to isolate what is essential—what is our essence—and thus what it means to be so that being matters. There may be no preestablished method that guarantees success; but once again the possibility-within-the-actual is irresistible: we do have factual inquiries on our shelves that are manifestly worthy of being carried out. This fact by itself cannot satisfy us, but it can and does bar the foreclosure of inquiry into worth by the warrant of relativism.

Nevertheless the adjectives *worthy* and *great* are not without their difficulties. What kind of reasoning, if any, can provide authority to such judgment? Perhaps access to our own meaning, and hence our worth, as well as the worth of the asking itself, is to be found in the very nature of self-reflection; but if so, such discovery is itself illuminated by irony. Perhaps reason in its earliest stage, as Schopenhauer suggests, really is nothing else than a tool in the service of utility: we find ourselves succeeding in everyday concerns if we think coherently about such things; hence we deem it worthwhile to develop our ability to reason. Soon, however, the mere use of reason becomes a kind of end in itself: we take satisfaction simply in solving problems, thinking ourselves clever if, as debaters, we are equally skillful in affirming and denying the same position. This skill, however, is profoundly misological;

its very success teaches us that eristic reasoning is entirely worthless since both sides of a dispute can be equally argued, leaving us worse off than we began. This is the cruel irony. But awareness *that* such misology occurs when reason is unanchored to truth, itself requires a reflective transcendence, which, in a way, exiles our breath with the stunning of its revelation, and this breathlessness becomes a laughter at our folly, and hence is a comedic, redemptive irony. The worth of questions can indeed be determined, and not by reference solely to their consequences or even to their answers. The penetrative depth of refined asking is of worth just because *depth* here means nearing or approaching the core, the essence, the fundamental ground from which all other evaluations must spring. We know we can be distracted by trivial asking about the most serious and weighty problems: love, duty, suffering, death, honor, justice. The topics are worthy in the way we *ask* about them being worthy. Hence, the way of asking itself matters; but how to determine such quality in asking is not resolvable by some prior algorithm or method. Every worthy asking always carries with it a critique of method, not as a negativist skepticism doubting it can be done, but an openness to discovery that learns how we ask even as it asks about what is asked.

The dismissal of the debater's misology is necessary, but there is a persistence of its enmity in other forms. We may launch this effort by asking Are philosophical questions unanswerable? If we say yes, they are unanswerable, then it seems such inquiry is folly, for why ask if no answer is possible? If, however, we say no, such questions are answerable, then we seem committed to either a permanent frustration of endless waiting for an answer that never comes, or stumbling somehow on the answer, in which case philosophy ceases, Lessing notwithstanding. There are meaningless questions which are recognized *as* meaningless just because they cannot be answered. We say the question, "Is red heavier than blue?" is meaningless because it cannot be answered: weight has no role in distinguishing color. These childish examples, however, may be distracting. Kant's analysis of the first two antinomies shows that to ask when the world began or whether there is a smallest particle are meaningless questions because they, too, are unanswerable. To realize they are unanswerable, however, requires considerable analysis and concentration. It is not intuitively obvious they are meaningless: they must be shown by prodigious effort to be unanswerable. If unanswerability is that condition which determines a question as meaningless, and if we insist that philosophical questions are never resolved, then, by this reasoning, is not philosophy meaningless? We sense uneasily that this analysis must be flawed; and indeed it is; but unless this flaw is exposed the unease remains a canker. A few points should be made at the onset.

First, to say that philosophical questions are entirely unanswerable is false, though to say they are unanswerable entirely is true. Philosophers do make contributions to our understanding of the great questions, and in many ways these contributions are both more certain and more spectacular than responses in other disciplines. Such contributions may not produce a complete satisfaction for all the dimensions of our questioning (they are not answerable entirely), but they can and sometimes do provide genuinely satisfying and irreversible discoveries (they are entirely answerable). Second, it should be pointed out that no discipline is answerable entirely: as the nuclear physicist gets ever smaller units to play with, there is always the next generation waiting to find even smaller units. No efficient cause in any discipline is complete, since the cause identified requires yet another cause as yet unidentified. Such lack of closure may irritate comfortable minds, but it does not in the least disqualify the legitimacy of our limited discoveries. Science works even if it is still incomplete. This scientific incompleteness may be due to the sheer complexity of nature; if so, it is entirely unlike philosophical incompleteness, which rests not on the complexity of the phenomena studied, but on the very nature of asking as self-reflective inquiry. Third, the nature of philosophical questioning marks its success not by terminating answers but by a deepening of our understanding. We need not discard a profound revelation about the nature of suffering or courage merely because there may be more to think about, or even if the revelation itself opens up new levels of questioning. Fourth, and finally, it is yet true that, just as there can be no answer without at least an implied question, so there can be no asking without the understanding of a possible justification for asking, which is usually thought of as an answer, but can, and should in philosophy, be thought of as truth. Unless truth both matters and is possible, there can be no genuine asking of any sort, much less fundamental asking. The point revealed in this inquiry into inquiry is that truth is available not only in the answer but also in the asking—that indeed, given the close interconnection, the very difference between asking and answering begins to break down, though never entirely. Answers are themselves revealed as questions and questions are revealed as answers.

We may consider an example of supreme and prodigious philosophical asking. How, Kant asks, are synthetic a priori judgments possible? This single question altered the history of philosophy; and even now thoughtfully to ask it may send a shiver of profundity down the spine. The question does not, however, pop out full blown from Zeus's head, or the undergraduate's. We first must learn what synthetic a priori judgments are, and why they seem so unlikely; and learning that, we must concentrate before we can realize how the fact of their occurrence, and hence their possibility, challenges the naive epistemology that precedes their discovery. Even with all this propaedeutic, however, the enormity of the single question is not appreciated until it brings us face to face with an even greater confrontation with our reasoning: the antinomies. If we read the correspondence with his friends during the ten years of gestation from 1770 to 1780, we realize that, in Kant's own personal journey of the critical method, what initiated his work on the *Critique* was his realization of the antinomies. Working from the antinomies, backward, he discovered the internality of the connective principles—which alone allowed him to confront antinomic thinking without contradiction. The internality of the principles of connection thus allowed him to focus on the paradox of this great truth: only by means of internal rules can we gain access to external phenomena, as a pair of glasses allows the visually impaired to see the world more clearly—or even, as the world "really" is. Only with this insight was Kant enabled to discover—and we note this with some amusement—how to ask the great question about synthetic a priori judgments. In his own inquiry, the great question emerged almost at the end; but it was his genius that spotted it *as* the question. We who read it may sense vaguely at the onset how important the question is, but even we, guided by the structured inquiry of the text, learn the full significance of the question only when the dialectic dazzles us with its sublime synthesis. Kant's critique is a species of fundamental asking; yet his question itself does not strike us at first as that revealing. How we make certain judgments with funny names surely is not as fundamental as asking about the origin of the universe or why God seems to care about man as echoed in David's psalm. Indeed, the question itself is not fundamental: it is the penetrative asking that proceeds from the question that is fundamental, forcing us to re-ask all the great questions from God and suffering, to freedom and finitude. The point is that even in this tiny sketch, the lines between answers and questions are blurred. Only the most dedicated reader is able, after much labor, to know what is being presupposed, what is being analyzed, what is being asserted, and what is being asked and re-asked. Even internal to the analysis are questions raised in a paradoxical or even ironic way: we need a pure intuition to ground empirical intuitions. But is not a pure intuition itself a paradox? How can I represent an object before it becomes an object? Kant *wants* us to feel this puzzlement: without it the transcendental discovery is not learnable. Perhaps there is even a sense of the comic when we realize how adroitly Kant uses the technique of paradox: it *seems* such things as pure intuition and synthetic a priori judgments are impossible. Is this not a conjurer's technique, making the utterly simple seem impossible, thereby dazzling the audience? Perhaps. But in philosophical conjury, the simple is revealed as simple only by means of the honest dazzling of our reflective reasoning. There may be nothing more obvious, more banal, more irresistibly true, than my own existence. It is the questioner who takes this simple banality, and by learning new and troubling questions to ask, turns it into a profound radiance. Of course I exist, so what? But I need not exist. So, why should I exist rather than not? What does it mean for me to exist, being contingent? The obvious answer has become a profound question.

Inquiry is, definitionally, an asking; but not all inquiry is philosophical. Science can also inquire, and indeed profoundly, though perhaps not fundamentally. There is a curse in the very prolixity of uses for the term *science*. Some of these uses, though they will never be expunged from the vernacular argot, should be quarantined by the precise, or at least belled like the cat, with warnings. To speak of scientific knowledge, for example, is ambiguous. Does it mean the knowledge, now recognized as facts, achieved by scientific inquiry? This troubles us because all facts seem to qualify, in some sense, as "science." It is a scientific fact that objects fall to the ground. Or is it scientific only if gravity as an explanation is included? There were various ancient theories about gravity: Are such theories nonscientific merely because they were replaced by a seemingly superior account? We also speak loosely of *the* scientific method, as if there were only one. If science is the testing of hypotheses by experimentation, we really should not use the term to describe the results, but only the testing itself; but even this refinement seems to leave out the most important step; how do we hypothesize at all? Not all hypotheses are deserving of the label *scientific*—empty speculations on the nature of the universe are not necessarily scientific just because they cannot be disproved. For the sake of the present reflections, these vagaries may be shelved provisionally by restricting our attention to the question: What does it mean to inquire as a scientist?

If asking is essential to inquiry, and all asking presupposes some knowledge as well as some scheme of coherence which gives a rational basis to the asking, we then can suggest that the schemes of coherence in science are what we call hypotheses. And the presupposed knowledge is not the new discoveries the hypothesis may make available, but the already existing knowledge that either leads the scientist to project a scheme to make the isolated data already available cohere, *or* provides the scientist with hints or cues that enable a judgment to be made about future discovery. This disjunct is of crucial significance, and is often overlooked. The sensitive, experienced lab director may be able to make nonalgorithmic judgments about which experiments should be made, and this power of judgment, perhaps akin to aesthetic judgment, may be of immense value to the lab. Such judgments are not the same as making up a scheme to provide coherence to disparate items of information. There can be no doubt that this judging is essential to science, yet is distinct from the projecting of hypotheses. They may, of course, overlap, so that the judgment of how to proceed may determine the actual character of the hypothesis. The history of science often confuses the two: Was it judgment or hypothesis that led Madame Curie to speculate about what happened on the plates? That such a question is a challenge to our thinking in no way rids us of the need to make the distinction—indeed the challenge requires it. For the moment it is enough to suggest that judgments depend on the unique, nonshareable character of the judge, whereas hypotheses do not depend on this character.

For now our focus is elsewhere. Earlier, in the account of ordinary questioning, it was noted that asking the time assumes the scheme provided by clocks, and thus the asking itself brings this particular scheme forward or makes it explicit, thereby providing coherence on the level of possibility to the actual, true answer: three o'clock. In science, however, the new scheme is not so much assumed, but raised itself *as* a question. There must still be presumed or assumed schemed coherence, that precedes and hence enables the asking, but what is being raised is a more explicit scheme, and hence is not a mere quest for more data, but a scheme of coherence. How are such schemes, now entertained as hypotheses, possible? Surely this possibility does not rest solely within our power to imagine things, for the number of such imaginings are limitless, and of themselves offer no reason for one being better than the other. If the radical egalitarianism of schemes were testable only by externalist experimentation, we would still be hunting with stones and spears. It is sometimes argued that the Baconian emphasis on experimentation opened the floodgates of "the" modern scientific method, but this view is both historically false—since many experimenters lived prior to Bacon—and more important, misrepresents how science asks its questions. Another way to make this point is to focus briefly on the vagueness of the term *experimentation.* We experiment already within the limited coherence of a scheme, even if that scheme is as simple as the techniques of isolation, in which the "experiment" is nothing else than the control of the environment to allow differentiation. The isolation, as well as the technique of isolating, however, are never independent of hypothetical asking which provides, even if vaguely, a scheme of coherence. The sharp division between experiment and hypothesis must thus be blurred, but not entirely broken down. Could it be that the success of the Baconian revolution—if such a thing really took place— be not the greater reliance on external experiment but more profoundly a new way of considering or raising hypotheses? After Bacon we hypothesize in terms of possible experimentation; we seek coherence in the possibility of the *actual.* Our knowledge of the history of science shows us that many of the great discoveries of the last three centuries were not the result of controlled experiment, but the result of reflective asking of an especially profound kind.

History of science however, being anecdotal, cannot be our central focus. The nature of scientific inquiry—and how it differs from philosophical inquiry—is. The suggestion is that the traditional difference—that science has an externalist, experimental component or even basis denied the philosopher—is incorrect; rather, the difference lies in how the asking takes place. We note that all inquiry, as inquiry, must include the asker as part of its coherence; and this requirement seems at first glance to disqualify science, except on the rare occasions when the observer or the observation itself becomes a part of the equation, as Heisenberg shows. These occasions, however, seem so atypical that to consider them as essential seems unwarranted. Yet, it may be that Heisenberg-type inclusions of the observer are only explicit recognitions of what is implicit in all inquiry. Certainly the topic of a given science is not what matters: psychology, sociology, and anthropology may take the human species as the central datum of analysis, but they are not, by this account, accorded the rank of scientific paradigm. Indeed the suspicion is deep that treating human beings as specimens in vast cultural laboratories violates both the truth of humanity and the propriety of science. Even evolutionary biology, which perforce must include the human species, does not thereby catch the role or nature of the inquirer as part of the inquiry, for we are not rendered coherent merely by our membership in our species. In spite of these caveats, however, it is yet possible to maintain that a part of science, perhaps only in its rarer achievements of greatness, can genuinely inquire—that is, include the inquirer as part of the inquired.

Even when science does inquire, however, it is dissimilar from philosophy in the nature of its asking. Hypotheses, as ways of asking, seek to provide coherence *as schematic,* even when the thinker belongs in that scheme;

philosophy does not provide but discovers reflective coherence, not in schemes but in the reality of the self being in the real world. To be sure, some philosophers mistakenly assert that their inquiry is indeed projected as a scheme, and some scientists avow that they do not use schemes, but find coherence in what is real; but there is no reason to accept their self-evaluations merely because they assert it. If either thinker contributes greatly to their discipline—an event more likely in the sciences than in philosophy, given the fundamental misunderstanding of their endeavors—we are quite willing to learn from them without accepting their misapprehension about inquiry. Nevertheless, the scientific inquirer's persuasion that his asking is rooted in something more real than mere imagined schemes of coherence is correct; and not merely because these schemes refer to, and illuminate, actual events. It is rather because these schemes are not merely imagined—they are also learned. This does not render them unschematic, but merely that what is uncovered in the inquiry reveals the truth about how nature works.

On the one hand, theoretical scientists are rightfully chary of stepping into metaphysics. They know too well the history of their own discipline, and the fall of previous theories that had been accepted as final and are now transcended by new revelations. Such demise of past theories, however, is deemed to belong to the actual enterprise of science. On the other hand, this caution, particularly in the present era, has perhaps become ungoverned. Talk about paradigms, alternative theories, speculative possibilities, "making up" hypotheses or even "perspectives," now dominates the language, giving an unhealthy relativism to what is far more reliable than that. Darwin's discovery of natural selection and Einstein's of the relativity of space and time have both curiously, and falsely, created, by their very success, a mistrust of absolutes altogether. Neither of these monumental achievements is in the least destructive of absolutist truth, any more than is quantum physics or even Heisenberg's so-called indeterminacy.

Both relativity and natural selection originate in genuine inquiry rather than mere analysis because both, whether consciously or not, reflect critically on the very nature of our thinking, and hence include the thinker in what is being thought. In the case of relativity we are asked to suspend our natural inclination to see space and time as constants, and instead shift the constancy to the speed of light. In doing so, how we think is radically recentered, producing what at first seem utterly weird possibilities. Does a six-feet tall man, rocketing upward at half the speed of light, "really" become three feet tall? The adverb is now crucial: not *really*, but mathematically, since, after all, space and time are now relative notions. We can conceive them *as* relative, however, only *as* mathematical; but now the mathematics is statistical, and hence nonspecific. This, however, changes what mathematics itself means, and hence is self-reflective in an important sense. Rethinking the nature of the scientist as mathematician turns out to enable us to think more profoundly about phenomena; though it must be added that it also opens up a scabrous license to abuse such language. Natural selection also has this reflective aspect, not only in the obvious point about our own species being the result of such machinations, but far more important, in what happens when such thinking includes the actual practitioner. Immunologists, for example, observe the actual mutations of the host organisms by the invading organisms. What they call "natural immune systems" refer to the ability of the host organism to resist these incursions with considerable, though not absolute, success. However, by their observations, the immunologists can add their own reasoning and intelligence to develop pharmaceutical support to enhance the defensive strategies of the host organism. This, however, curiously, makes the community of thinking immunological scientists an extension of immunity itself. Once this happens, the notion of "natural immune systems" no longer is sufficient: such systems become "assisted natural immune systems," in which the assistance comes from reflective thinking. These instances show that science can be genuine inquiry and not merely the projection of hypothetical schemes onto testable phenomena. Nevertheless, they yet require schemes of coherence rather than the reality of the self in the real world, and because of this they lack many of the characteristics of fundamental asking, such as surprise, hearing, paradox and irony; but above all they do not possess the four qualities listed at the beginning of this chapter as essential for philosophical inquiry.

It is, however, the point made just prior to the detour on science that is most critical. We noted, briefly, that the brute reality of my own contingent existence confronts me with a peculiarly revealing kind of question. Granted that I exist, it is not necessary that I exist; so my existence is somehow a bestowal in some sense. It is possible, perhaps even needful, to consider one remarkable response to this contingency: I may be grateful for it. Certainly there is gratitude in David's psalm. There is much wealth to be mined from the ore of this phenomenon, and the drift of the present inquiry now seems to make imperative a direct questioning of what it means to be grateful.

8

Gratitude

What does it mean to wonder about the world? Some of us are able to find endless satisfaction in marking the marvels within the world. We watch in fascination the remarkable development of crystals, and wonder why we do not say they are alive. We study with great pleasure the behavior and habitats of the wolf, the whales, the radiant butterfly. We amaze ourselves in noting the social activities of people in cities, on the farms, or bent in silent contemplation in stone, cold abbeys. We ponder the whores in the streets, the young on the killing fields. We wonder at the youthful body healing itself all on its own, without our intrusion. No part of the world seems without its fervid and fervent observers, taking odd pleasure in the difficult learning that adds so much not only to our knowledge but to our delight. These are but parts of the world. Some note them, others do not. How does it differ to wonder about them and to wonder about the world itself? The lover finds his interest entirely captive by his one, single beloved; no movement she makes is unworthy of his eye, no secret learned about her moods, her smiles, her body glorious, can be disregarded. The rest of the world fades into a mere frame whose sole function is to enclose this radiant artwork wrought by nature, ineffably his. Are not all these precious concerns similar to beloved paintings, enframed by the otherwise jejune moldings we call the world? Who but a fool admires the frame above the picture? Romeo does not love everyone, he loves only Juliet; and he is, because of this singular passion, yclept the greatest lover of them all. To love is to select; to love all is to love none; if everyone is my brother no one is my brother. Is not wondrous asking of the world akin to the vacuity of loving everyone, since love just means treating as special? If the world itself is wondrous, and the world is all there is, then nothing is unwondrous, and so we say nothing to say it is wondrous since wonder loses its significance when nothing can be excluded from it.

If we mean by the world the mere enclosure of all that is, perhaps it is not wondrous; but if we mean by the world where we dwell, where we belong, its mere ubiquity does not forfeit the possibility of wonder. There is a knotty problem here, best revealed by Kant in his stunning analysis of the first two antinomies. We can ask, he says, about beginnings and causes of everything within the world, but we cannot ask about the origin, size, or cause of the world itself, since all such thinking, as it provides connectives, must presuppose the world. We cannot say the world begins, since all beginning begins in the world; but neither can we say the world has no beginning, since this claim is merely the negation of the previous one, and it, too, presupposes the world. Kant's critique is entirely sound. Some thinkers, however, abuse this premium of thought by saying that the world is thereby rendered entirely unavailable for any thinking; it is the mysterious thing-in-itself, lurking behind our perceptions. The point is far less mysterious: efficient causal explanations in time and space are not applicable to the world, but this merely limits the range and efficacy of such explanation. We can still ask what it means to be in the world, and we can ask this precisely and only because we are in it. There is no need for an externalist perspective outside the world; such a suggestion would indeed abuse the critical analysis given by Kant.

This perhaps relieves us of existential nihilism, but the problem persists: How do we ask such questions? and What does it mean to ask them? Is there philosophical magic in the word *dwell* that, when chanted like a mantra, salves the burning of our wonder? One might well object that, just as in the case of cause, we always dwell within an area or space that is a local habitation, a part of the world, not all of it. To ask what it means to dwell in ancient Athens, biblical Jerusalem, or medieval Paris is meaningful precisely because Athens is not Jerusalem, the Greek culture is different from the Hebrew or Christian culture; so to move from these local centers to the world is as invalid as moving from specific causes in the world to the cause of the world. There is, it seems, no world culture, only local culture. The disanalogy here is profound. The local cultures reflected by Athens, Jerusalem, and Paris are meant not to tell their inhabitants about the Greeks, the Hebrews, or the French, but about the world. For David, dwelling in Jerusalem was dwelling in the world, including the non-Hebraic parts, for the local, cultural belonging provided him with the piety necessary to open up the world in such a way as to move us, dwelling in the twenty-first-century American habitation, with a universal—world-embracing—passion. There is a paradox here, but a dear one. The Greek Xenophanes noted this as well. The realization that the Thracian gods had red hair and the Egyptian gods had dark hair did not move Xenophanes to cultural relativism, as it does lesser, contemporary thinkers, but to monotheism. David was not so foolish as to believe that only Israel existed, that Egypt was an illusion; nor was he unwilling to learn from cultural contacts outside his homeland; but neither was he so foolish as to believe that the Egyptian's denial of the "one true God" meant that his piety was false, or that it was merely one alternative among many. The intensity of his local advocacy is necessary for universal truth, which is why his psalms still move us not only because of their beauty but because of their truth. A relativist David could not sing like that. No relativist ever can sing like that.

   It may seem that dwelling in the world is impossible since the nondweller—the exile—must also be in the world. The foreign is needful for there to be a home. If by *world* is meant the ultimate spatial container, and *home* and *away* are merely separate parts of that container, and if we dwell only at home, this criticism would be fatal: we could not dwell in the world. But both *dwell* and *world* are, in this criticism, assigned purely geographical meanings, not existential ones. The argument is not that everyone dwells equally in the world. Dwelling is something at which we can succeed or fail. It is a way of being in the world which only the thoughtful asker can achieve; and it is only as dwellers in the world that fundamental asking can occur. The non-asker may be able to achieve local dwelling if he develops the genuine virtue of piety, but only as asker can this local piety provide access to the world as dwelling place. Fundamental asking familiarizes the vast; the world becomes our home—that is, we can dwell in the world rather than merely in our local place—only because our local piety prisms the multitudinous colors into a single, white beam. This metaphoric prism, however, cannot be achieved by abstract generality, for it is not a process by which we extract in our imagination certain common elements from otherwise diverse particulars. Rather it recognizes universality within fiercely held local advocacy. We can ask fundamentally only because within our own private or local passion can we discern the universality that is fundamental. Indeed, it turns out that this confronting of the universal in the fierce devotion to the local is what fundamental asking is. Asking is not some other thing we can do in the environment of localized universality; fundamental asking is contained already in this confronting.

In earlier chapters we noted the priority of the possible-within-the-actual over mere conceptual or modal possibility. We now must recognize the necessary-within-the-actual, in which the necessary is shifted from the pure formality of modal logic to the existential sense of concrete universality, discerned in the phenomenon of dwelling within the world. Universality need not always entail the necessary existence of something—as, for example, we might admit the universal truth that courage requires a struggle within oneself, without claiming that there must be actual courageous people. The necessity is therefore not that there is courage or struggle but that what it means for there to be courage necessarily contains what it means to struggle. Universality of meaning entails existential necessity: I *must* think in a certain way about courage in order to understand what courage means, hence the universality of such understanding entails the necessity of thinking in this way. Concrete universality, such as is contained in a great artwork or in a heroic figure can become a resource for learning and hence truth, as *King Lear* reveals the truth about what it means to be denied gratitude. Artworks, however, even though they obviously reveal universal and hence existentially necessary truths are always rooted in a local culture; great figures in history, such as the adversaries Lincoln and Robert E. Lee, are both fierce defenders of local advocacy, but their brilliance and eloquence transform their advocacy into universality available to those not sharing their parochial interests. The concrete, local struggles of Lincoln and Lee, through the necessity locked into the existential universality of what these struggles mean, become sources of learning that are noncontingent. It is not obvious that all who struggle provide in their struggle such universal meaning, so we are not speaking merely of examples under a general rule. If Lincoln would have appealed abstractly to the concept of patriotism, the crowd at Gettysburg and the alert world press would have noted it not at all.

This may seem to labor at the obvious. Few would deny that local advocates at times strike universal chords whether wittingly or no, and this majority need not worry at all about necessity within the actual. What most thinkers find troubling is not that particular individuals within a local culture may reveal truths that transcend the culture, but that the local advocacy is a necessary element in such truth. Why even consider the local culture at all? If Lincoln is correct in saying that, in a legal or even moral sense, all are created equal, why must the American culture matter to the non-American listener who may recognize the truth of such a claim? At best, one might say, America is merely a fleeting example of that truth. Lincoln's passion for the American union, sponsored by the ideas noted in the whole speech, and not merely the isolated idea of equality, is not merely a personal account of his private feelings, but is a part of the truth itself. This captive of thought must be tortured to reveal its secret.

A clue might be found in the dramatic unfolding of Plato's *Republic*. First, there are citizens, whose virtue is *sophrosune;* then there are warriors, whose virtue is courage; and then, chosen only from among the most gifted warriors, are the rulers, who have learned to develop the virtue of wisdom. Why must the rulers be chosen only from the warriors? Why need the warriors be a special class anyway? Socrates tells us that this tripartite state is mirror of the tripartite soul: appetite, spirit, and mind. Why do we need spirit? Is it not possible for an ordinary citizen, not a warrior, to be blessed with superior intelligence, who might well add luster and insight sitting on the elect senate of rulers? Socrates does not deny there may be gifted non-warriors more intelligent and insightful than the select ex-warriors. He does deny, however, that, lacking warrior-spirit, such a man belongs on the ruling senate; for intellect without spirit is mere intelligence, not true wisdom. The spirit of the warrior is a species of local advocacy or piety: without it the brilliant bureaucrat or tyrant may be possible, but not the virtuous ruler. Contemporary superstition clearly denies this; indeed the present mode of thought finds this Socratic insistence on pious education of the guardians entirely dangerous. It is not only not necessary but not desirable to have a local education in which the virtues, especially piety, are taught. For, these critics argue, it is precisely the local virtues that constitute the impediments to universality: they are, as local, inevitably prejudicial, bigoted, chauvinistic, and intolerant. The heroes of the unenlightened past, such as the priest, the parent, the pious, and the patriot, are today depicted in the popular arts and classrooms either as wicked villains or pathetic rubes, scorned in the mockery of disdain or juvenile indifference. In such an atmosphere it is extremely difficult to find much sympathy for the Socratic education in the *Republic* which replaces the more "acceptable" education of the slave-boy in the *Meno*. But this populist disdain for Plato's insistence on spirit as essential to the soul need not deter philosophical truth-seekers. It is enough merely to note the environment of hostility to the notion in order to help clarify what is at issue. Necessity-within-the-actual is not found in an iso-lated individual but in culturally localized dwelling from which we speak in local tongues about universal truths. There is, of course, no "pure," culture-less individual; even—or especially—the most rabid revolutionary or non-conformist is identified in terms of the culture putatively being denied. Rather than being a negativistic impediment, local advocacy or culture is the only legitimate stairwell to the heights of universality.

It is when this local advocacy is intensified with the singular passion for truth as intrinsically worthy that fundamental asking occurs. Abstract uni-versality cannot provide the world as a dwelling, and mere acceptance of a local tradition cannot move us beyond either a frightened or an unmarked security. It is not knowledge that is so passionately thought, but truth; all that is known must perforce be true, but truth is not always encased in knowledge. The reverential hearing of that which surprises us in its truth is not the enclosing act which is the assertion of knowledge but the opening act which asks in awesome gratitude. A fierce sense of our own worthless-ness outside of fundamental dwelling is echoed not in the desire to know, revered as this may be, but that we, undeserving, are nevertheless welcome. "Who are we?" becomes not a request for knowledge of a proper label, i.e., the listing of necessary and sufficient conditions, but "who are we *that . . . ?*" Who are we that we should matter? Not mattering seems necessarily a gen-uine possibility; so, that we *do* matter seems a bestowal impossible to achieve entirely on our own. Mattering, though essential, may distract by its puta-tive axiological basis (which makes *mattering* not matter very much); so we dig more deeply to recognize that we can ask, Who are we that we should *be?* Our being is surely contingent, so to be at all is a bestowal in the pres-ence of which we must listen in surprise, discover our enablement in the pos-sibility within our own actuality, and confront the universality within the actuality of our dwelling in the world. To ask why we matter—what is the worth of our non-necessary existence?—is impossible if we are but elements or parts within a container-world. If we insist on seeing ourselves merely as parts within a vast, indifferent universe, we can only conclude one of two things: either our existence is entirely fortuitous—it just happened that way—or it is necessary as a purely logical function of an entirely determined universe conceived solely as nature. Neither of these cosmological hypothe-ses permits even raising the fundamental questions of our worth or why we should be in the world, or even what the world means. To be able to be as enabling possibility may (dangerously) be called freedom; to be universally enabled by our actuality may (dangerously) be called piety or dwelling. The parenthetical dangers are obvious: if we see freedom merely as the moral species of causality and piety merely as local indoctrination for which affection arises out of habit, the existential authority of this insight is entirely lost.

Freedom rightly has been identified by many thinkers, especially Kant, as necessary for the attribution of responsibility. It is sometimes reduced to this: to be free means being able to be held responsible, both by one's self and by others. The first claim is defensible, the second is not. Freedom does provide for responsibility, but is not reducible to it. Being free suggests a special, internal awareness of the preciousness of my own existence—a kind of character-integrity, if you will, so that who I am matters—without which freedom would ascribe censure or praise to a purely formal, empty notion, itself without meaning. How can I be responsible unless who I am first matters? The temptation is to say that what makes me matter is nothing more or less than my being able to be responsible. But this turns out to be a redundancy: I am responsible because I am responsible. The term *responsible* swallows the *I* in one gulp of reductionist reasoning. A similar threat lurks behind piety. It may dangerously be seen merely as a certain heuristic advantage in the training of children, and apparently the continuance of a certain mythical bonding among less than stellar adults too stupid to achieve independence of thought. Without piety, however, I can at best be in the world; I cannot belong or dwell in it; but unless I dwell in the world there can be no existential universality, and hence there could be no freedom either. Piety is possible only for adults, for it recognizes not merely the power of law but also its magnificence.

We often note this phenomenon. Obedience to the law begins with simple fear of its might: to disobey is to face punishment. From obsequious adherence to the precepts there may then develop a certain resentment, that, among the powerless, may grow darkly to a seething hatred, all the more cancerous for its impotence. Nietzsche identifies this as a necessary step in the genealogy of morals, represented by the slave morality of the priestly class. From these dark haters may emerge a few rebels who constitute the seeds of revolution. But this genealogy is by no means inevitable. A more benign development can be seen when, the adolescent anger and resentment being spent, there emerges a love of the institution, for all its faults. We obey the laws not only because they are right, but because they are ours, thereby responding to the numbing questioning in the *Euthyphro.* Indeed, among the remarkable are those willing to obey even some dubious laws out of affection for their origin. It is perhaps inevitable that Eve must rebel against God's enigmatic prohibition against knowledge of good and evil; but after her achieved freedom, it is possible that she regrets offending God, not because of the law, but because of her love. So many pacificists against the First World War, such as Bertrand Russell and Albert Einstein, became militant patriots in the Second. Did they change their view? Not really: they may well be indicted of a dangerous naivete, but they saw the first conflict as a danger to what was their own in the war; they saw in the second conflict a danger to what was their own in the peace. Steven Decatur, Robert Lee, Captain Vere in *Billy Budd*, and Socrates in the *Euthyphro*, all manifest a nonchildish affection for what is their own; perhaps none so eloquently as Stephen Orbelian's simple: "I love my country because it is mine." Such patriotic affection supercedes the mere fear of punishment that may have been a necessary propaedeutic for a love that surpasses moral understanding. In this genealogy, as opposed to Nietzsche's, slavelike fear becomes, in maturity, an existential piety, so that piety surpasses the fear rather than being identified with it.

These anecdotal reflections show that freedom is not merely a moral notion. They also suggest that piety enables the local to become universal. Only the pious can be free, and only the free can be pious. It is not by dropping our pious concerns for what is our own that we achieve universality, as if the concrete impedes the truth about the world; for this disregard of what is our own achieves a mere formal abstraction that is "universal" only because it lacks content. The realization that our mere geographical location within the limitless expansion of space cannot provide any understanding of the world demands that we see the world concretely as the ground of our belonging. Those blind to the truths revealed in local advocacy are not simply in another place, believing in their own local gods that are mere alternatives to what is ours; they are lacking. We ourselves may also be lacking, but not because alternative cultures are equally worthy or true, but because our piety about the locally rooted universal truths may itself be shallow, or distorted by fears and prejudice, or because fear may impede the critical from refining what is ours.

The welcome offered by our home, when reflected on, surprises us because there is no moral right to it. Deprived of accounting for this welcome by moral reasoning, the courageous dig more deeply, and discover that there is no common account; that whatever enables the welcome is rooted in the deepest origin of our essence and the essence of the world. This discovery is not of a species of knowledge but of asking—it is truth mattering on its own, and hence it leads to fundamental asking. When we ask fundamentally, we are therefore confronting the truth in its most original form:

Why do we belong in the world at all? What is the world that we belong in it? Who are we that the world is our dwelling? We cannot respond to these questions merely with propositions; what makes the questions meaningful is what it means to ask them: gratitude.

The essence of ingratitude is either the plerophry that all advantage is mine by right, or that all such advantage is merely fortuitous. We note the malignancy of the former in Shakespeare's depiction of the "pelican daughters" of King Lear, in Dante's vision of the lowest place in hell as reserved for ungrateful traitors, in the political paralysis that follows from the inflation of putative "rights," and the emasculation of ungoverned egalitarianism beyond the legal demand for it. We note it when parents abuse their children by denying privilege and a sense of gratitude, when a culture is embarrassed to celebrate its own worth, when greatness is disdained as arrogance, and vulgarity is condoned on the basis of nonintervention. If all advantage is mine by right, any lack is a lugubrious, doleful blot on the machinery of existence. The reduction finally reaches its own absurdity: I have a right to existence: I *ought* to have been born; all disadvantage is therefore a usurpation, so since the world always seems to withhold something, the world itself is hated for being a cheat. If this seems rather silly, the reason is because it is silly.

The other alternative denying gratitude is that advantage and disadvantage are not calculable; they are sheer fortuity, and as such cannot even be thought about. It may be true that advantage and disadvantage cannot always be calculable, but that we are thereby deprived of any rational resource to deal with them in any way embarrasses. Why be reasonable at all if this, my highest faculty, is worthless where most it is needed? Why be wealthy if, being rich, I am ashamed to buy unnecessary or superfluous things? Is that not precisely what wealth is *for?* Analogously, if we cannot think about what it means to be welcome, or to have gracious bestowals, or simply to be glad I am alive, then thinking is a sham. It may indeed be more difficult to probe the depths of our fate and the meaning of our existence than it is to figure out with the simple shepherd, Colin, that the great cause of the day is the sun. There is a craven security in limiting thought to what we already know works, and many philosophers suffer ill repute by mere codification of the obvious, or simply putting Greek terminology to everyday things, making them academic.

Do these reductions mean that fundamental asking is rooted in a mere emotional state: feeling thankful? All asking, of course, requires some species of what might be called emotional states: the desire to know, the itch of curiosity, the fear of danger or failure (as in the burning building), the love of wisdom (philosophy). Why is it then so unseemly to designate gratitude as an emotion, and thereby unworthy of having philosophical worth? Even so, these comparisons with desire and curiosity are misleading. Gratitude as the personal origin of fundamental asking is more akin to Kant's account of respect as the fundamental motive for the moral law. Kant's problem is that normal incentives seem to reduce both the dignity and the authority of the law, for if I merely *want* to know and obey the law, its compulsion seems weakened by its dependence on so arbitrary a motivation. (Suppose I do *not* want to know or obey the law. Is moral goodness, then, dependent merely on wanting?) Kant argues that respect is unlike most motives, for it partakes of both subjective and objective elements. It *is* a feeling, but a feeling based on our power to reason. This means law is not law unless it can be respected, and thus respect is unique among motives, given its authority. It is in some ways more than a motive, for it has an objective, rather than a subjective basis. Gratitude is to fundamental asking as respect is to the moral law and its originators. A thinker need not be highly motivated consciously by the *feeling* of gratitude in order to ask fundamentally any more than a reflective agent need have a powerful emotional sense of respect to appreciate the authority of the moral law. Those who have greater emotional feelings of respect or gratitude are thus not better morally nor better askers, though they may be more sensitive. It is necessary that these feelings provide access to the authority in each function, respect for agents capable of determining the moral law and gratitude for the world as my dwelling. Being grateful is thus more fundamental than feeling grateful, for gratitude originates in the authoritative consciousness of being in the world without having to be in the world, and realizing what this means.

One may, of course, regret one's existence. It is possible to grant that we contingently exist and wish we did not. Where gratitude is possible, so is ingratitude. It is even possible to suggest that one wrenched in the agony of wretched despair would raise the question of contingent existence as a curse, without the feeling of gratitude at all, and much philosophical insight might well emanate from such a conflict. This is akin to not wanting to know or obey the moral law. I still must, even though I greatly prefer not to, respect all agents, including myself, as originators of law. My regret at being cursed by unnecessary existence in a world I do not want to be in, in no way bars the authority of reflective gratitude. I may not respect one who deserves it. My not respecting such an agent, however, does not affect the legitimacy of the desert: he still *ought* to be respected whether I "feel" this or not. There is no moral obligation to feel grateful, for both the gracious (as bestower) and the grateful (as bestowed), by definition, are not reducible to moral obligation, else it would not be a bestowal at all. The point is not that we all *are* grateful, much less that we "feel" gratitude, but rather that only as gratitudinous can fundamental asking take place.

This comparison to respect suggests that gratitude, too, has a kind of authority to it that distinguishes it from other feelings and attitudes about our contingent existence. But comparing gratitude to respect for the moral law nevertheless raises an independent question, one which agonizes the inquirer even as it provides a deeper insight into the meaning of fundamental asking. This troubling, almost excruciating, problem may be identified as the paradox of gratitude. It is possible only now to confront it as a serious threat to fundamental asking.

A doting grandmother gives her favorite granddaughter a gift that pleases the child immensely. As her eyes light up with total delight, the little girl beams with unrestrained joy; the grandparent finds this response entirely satisfying, for her love of the child provides her with a sharing of the child's own happiness. Into this warm and radiant scene the girl's mother smilingly reminds her daughter that the grandmother should be thanked. Perhaps in this case the child readily and dutifully responds; but here lies a snag. Where does this "should" come from? Is the thanking required? If so, is it not a species of payment, the fulfilling of an obligation? The grandmother may even insist she is not looking for thanks; or that seeing her granddaughter's happiness is thanks enough. If the gift is a true bestowal, then why "should" or even "ought" the child give thanks? Perhaps the mother merely wants to use this moment as an opportunity to instill good manners in her daughter. It is merely "polite" to say "thank you"—a mere social custom. One may deem the child vulgar or unrefined if she does not respond gratefully. But why should this be so? What is vulgar about receiving a bestowal *as* a bestowal, needing no payment at all, not even thanks? Is it not a purer bestowal if done without expectation of being thanked? We must consider certain scenarios. Suppose the donor is repugnant to the recipient who may not even want the gift should it come from such a despised source. Need we say the recipient should nevertheless be grateful? Suppose, this repugnance being known, the donor bestows the gift on the beloved in such a way that the recipient is unaware of its source. Something akin to this happens to Pip in *Great Expectations*, though Pip does not find Magwitch repugnant. Should the recipient be required to be grateful to an unknown benefactor? This seems especially troubling if the recipient would be disgusted if the identity of this particular benefactor be known. Is this even *right:* to bestow a great gift secretly on one who, discovering the origins of the treasure would not accept it, or regret having accepted it? Is not the gratitude in such cases usurped?

Deeming thanks as a species of payment due is itself an ungracious judgment. I shall give you a gift if you will but thank me for it. Put so baldly the bargain seems crass. Yet, to bestow a gift and not be thanked, even if the thanks is not the reason for the bestowal, also seems crass. Huckleberry Finn claims the dollar found is better than the dollar earned—precisely, it seems, since the found dollar reflects the sheer favor of fate; we seem to matter, somehow, beyond our desert. But is a dollar found even better than a dollar *given?* If Huckleberry must uncomfortably do the right thing and thank someone for it, perhaps he would still prefer to find it, for then he need thank no one. There can be no doubt that at times being the recipient of excessive largesse can be a burden. This, however, may be due to the overly generous being thoughtless, or perhaps it marks the recipient as flawed. Socrates wisely points out to the boys in the *Lysis* that true friends never discuss money at all. The poor friend may be grateful for the friendship of his wealthier companion, but were he to express uneasiness at the expenditures that make possible their shared delights, the accompanying thanks may become insulting. The delicacy of judgment here may be one of the truest marks of a genuine friendship. The wealthier does not want his friend to feel indebted; the poorer does not want to seem ungracious. Yet, it is surely puritanical—and indeed ungracious—to refuse to allow wonderful things to happen only because they depend on the wealthier friend's exchequer. In Evelyn Waugh's *Brideshead Revisited,* the wealthy Sebastian Flyte taught his poorer friend, Charles Ryder, that such sabotage would itself be ungrateful. Socrates is right: true friends simply do not let the origin of the payments matter. This, however, seems even more outrageous: Is the poorer entirely ungrateful? We might also ask: Is not the richer friend grateful that his poorer friend not worry about who pays? It is perhaps enough that both the richer and the poorer are grateful for each other, a wisdom that celebrates the true glory of friendship. Yet friends do thank each other, and we consider it right and proper that they do. Ought we to thank? This still haunts us, for what does bestowal have to do with ought?

We rightly are aggrieved if, inviting friends out to dine at a costly restaurant, they insist on a reciprocity they cannot afford. We say they do not understand the nature of a gift; it is not commerce to be measured by mercantile exchange. At the same time we may shun as obsequious the profligacy of the overly generous, for too often we cannot resist the burden this puts on us, as if we owe a pseudo-gratitude—an indebtedness not freely taken—even if the giver makes no claim at all for recompense. If the gift be freely given, then is not the thanks also freely given, and hence not morally required at all?

Even as we suggest this, we reflect further: suppose a loving benefactor makes a huge sacrifice for one he holds dear and precious; the bestowal is accepted without any thanks at all; perhaps there is even disdain or contempt. Two responses seem possible. In the first we say that such ingratitude is a capital vice, and like the ungrateful in Dante's inferno, deserves the deepest torment. In the second we say the bestowals were from the unloved, we did not ask for them, and though they are desirable, gifts ought not be bargains for reluctant thanks; it is enough we accept them at all. Does not this follow from all these persuasions about the nonreciprocity of gifts? Or do we not mean what we say? I cannot be required to give a gift else it is not a gift but a social payment of dues. Why then must I be required to thank? Gift-giving and thanks-giving have this peculiar authority that they are not morally required yet they nonetheless are existential virtues that seem to make a demand on us, perhaps even greater than morality. We seem in suspense here, hanging torturously between the tendency to say we ought to give and thank, and the counter-tendency to say giving and thanking are worthy just because they are not compelled by ought. Suspense, though, belongs to the essence of asking.

What we thank in fundamental asking is the welcome of the world, by which I mean the enabling of my belonging in it. Without this enabling, neither the world nor our existence in it has any authority. No account of the species accounts for the individual if persons have any discrete meaning, for I cannot thank the species or bestow graciously on general concepts. To ask fundamentally is to recognize that we who ask wonder what it means that we, specific, unique persons, exist coherently—that is, thankfully—in the welcoming world.

The existential truth, sought solely for its own sake and not for some use or purpose, that reveals what it means contingently to exist, is available only in this torturous suspension made possible by thanking. This is fundamental because it reaches the unique essence: I do not thank because the species exists, but because I exist, and—note the contingency here—*if* I seek the truth of my own being solely for the sake of truth, I must celebrate my personal reality: this time; this place; these tastes; this love of this music and this friend; these challenges; this inheritance that gives me language to think with, art to enjoy, ironies to contemplate, and questions to ask; this fleeting life greeting this unshareable death; this preciousness that is unrepeatable yet bearing with it absolutely great authority—I am; I, thankfully, am.

To ask about something, even if it is about the entire world, in the ordinary ways of asking cannot ever include this authority inherent in our own unique existence, simply because ordinary asking is not, in its essence, gratitudinous. All asking, as asking, calls forth coherence; but in ordinary asking this coherence is provided by projected schemes. In fundamental asking the coherence is itself the reality of the asker dwelling in the real world as welcoming. Gratitude is thus fundamental coherence since it brings together what cannot be unified in any other way: my unique existence and my belonging to a local place that alone opens up the welcome to the entire world. No matter how elegant or profound, any mere scheme wrought to make sense of the entire world, as scheme, must fail to incorporate this central reality of the asker being in the world as grateful dweller.

The unfolding of this seemingly rambling chapter now takes on a certain authority. We note, first, that wondering about the world seems impossible, since normally what we wonder about is whatever is in the world. We then note that the seeming parochialism of local advocacy in fact can have universal meaning, which then allows local piety to provide for global piety, or belonging. It is then noted that there is a kind of universality-in-the-actual that is revealed when this piety is raised to the level of fundamental asking. Being able to be free, and hence responsible, requires an awareness that who we are matters; but this realization also shows that the worth which enables freedom, which is distinct from the worth that follows from freedom, is not earned or deserved but given, and thus is recognized *in its truth* only when the bestowal is affirmed. This affirmation is gratitude. There is no moral authority that requires that I exist, hence the way I must think about my own personal reality within the world is not approachable by what ought to be, though once I exist the moral has authority over me and bestows on me the rights inherent in being a responsible agent. If moral reasoning cannot illuminate what it means for me to be, my recognition of my bestowal as a unique being itself cannot be discovered in the authority of morality. Yet, in the paradox of gratitude neither can I deny that, in some sense, it is shameful not to be thankful for bestowals.

There is another facet to the paradox of gratitude. When a gift is given, not only is ingratitude shameful but so is its polar opposite, obsequious, fawning, false-humility, à la Uriah Heep. The analysis of why obsequy as well as ingratitude are offenses against bestowal is revealing. When I give a gift it is because I recognize and want to celebrate those existential qualities of the recipient that are the ground, in part, of my affection. For the recipient to assume the gift is his by right is ingratitude, to assume there is no basis at all is obsequy. It is an offense against the giver precisely because it undermines what the gift purports to show: the nonmoral worth which the affection, either friendship or love, reveals to the donor. To accept a gift graciously is, in a way, a countergift, for it says: I accept this because I am your friend, and though I have not *earned* the gift, I would not abuse the bestowal by denying precisely what you intend by the giving: that I am dear to you— amazing though this may be. It is a common enough fault among the lovesick that they assume they alone love, and we may take tender amusement when this occurs among the young especially—it seems to constitute the very stuff of the great comedies. For this reason, perhaps friends are better than lovers as models for analysis. Particularly in the exquisite attachments of youth, the healthy respect for one's own existential worth enables the unabashed sharing, sacrifice, and bestowals to occur glowingly in an intimacy that in many ways excels all others. What is shameful is for this glory to be sacrificed on the altar of self-debasement. All we need do is reflect upon the authentic giver's trust: he does not want his friend to sabotage the holiness of the bestowal either by the profanation of assuming it is earned or the sacrilege of denying that one's existential worth can matter.

A historical approach may further our grasp of this. Medieval Christians often seem to think that the baser they demote the human soul, the greater becomes the quality of their worship. So wretched are we that only the enormity of a divine sacrifice can redeem. All worth is found only in God; and we, radically unworthy, are unjustly saved from the eternal damnation we deserve only by grace. Though how an entirely worthless person can be said to *deserve* eternal punishment is beyond comprehension. Nietzsche quite rightly finds this self-debasement repulsive, calling it a species of slave-morality. But it is not only repulsive; it is inconsistent. We are accusing God of loving beings who are unlovable. These Christian-haters of themselves may argue that being loved or chosen or elect is the sole basis of why we are loved—that is, we are loved just because we are loved. Nietzsche, the archatheist should be thanked by any theist for pointing this out. Mention of this theological sacrilege of thought is made here in passing to show how profound the notions of gratitude and bestowal really are: they belong in our very understanding of ourselves in any existentially significant metaphysics.

Genuine gratitude therefore cannot depend on self-debasement precisely because the gift is given as a celebration of the nonmoral *worth* of the recipient; this worth must be nonmoral, for if it were moral it could not be the basis of bestowal but only of right. To treat bestowals as rights is recognized as a species of profanation; to treat bestowals as requiring self-debasing is sacrilege. Profanation is that assault on holiness from without (as the barbarians profane the holy temple) and sacrilege is the assault on holiness from within (as Judas betrays Christ or Claudius murders his kingly brother). Treating bestowals as rights is profane because the realm of grace is usurped or invaded by the externally moral; gratitude perverted by self-debasement is sacrilegious because the offense is within the realm of bestowal as a malignancy destroying the very possibility of grace whatsoever. Being grateful is not being ingratiated.

These precising concerns about the proper meaning of gratitude are of central importance to the possibility of fundamental asking. Whatever is gracious is necessarily transmoral, in the same sense that forgiveness is transmoral without being antimoral. In order for the transmoral to have any authority, it must be rooted in our confrontation of what it means to exist, and thus can be called existentially authoritative. Fundamental asking is fundamental because it confronts with authority the meaning of existence, and it is asking because this existence is confronted as non-necessary, or finite, and thus as a bestowal which can only be confronted gratefully as a way of asking.

If gratitude cannot, in its essence, be morally obligated then ingratitude cannot strictly be immoral; so we do not say we ought to thank. Being ungrateful is, however, shameful. The English language is richly endowed with a distinction not available in many other tongues: *should* is not as strong as *ought*. This allows us to suggest we should be grateful but not that we ought to be grateful. More helpful is the difference between shame and guilt: I am guilty when I violate a legal or a moral law, but I am ashamed when I diminish or want to diminish myself. Ingratitude is shameful; indeed doubly so since it shames me as well as the bestower. Curiously, the "weaker" *should* seems more compelling than the "stronger" *ought*, for I may shun the shame of ingratitude far more ardently than the guilt of immorality. Perhaps this is because I can be forgiven my immoral acts, but the shame of the ungraciousness itself erodes the possibility of forgiveness, since forgiveness is rooted in my existential worth, which is the same origin of grace. These helpful distinctions may save us from contradiction, but they do not remove the thorns inherent in the paradox of gratitude. We cannot help feeling some indebtedness to those who bestow on us undeserved favors; yet debt is precisely that moral onus which cannot belong to true bestowal or acceptance. It may take great courage to accept a gift as it is intended to be if it is a true bestowal—acceptance without indebtedness. What seems to be missing in most occasions is the full realization that thanking itself is a bestowal; that I the recipient must somehow rejoice in the existential worth that the donor sees in me without linking that worth to any right. The courage to accept bestowal may even be the greatest species of courage, because it demands an entirely nonarrogant pride. Perhaps this courage is itself a bestowal—a gift from ourselves to ourselves—making it both earned and bestowed, and hence the root of the paradox itself. In any event, this rare courage is needful for fundamental asking.

An overall sketch may here be helpful. The world cannot coherently be conceived as to omit our own reality as self-conscious persons. No purely natural explanation is able to provide this inclusion. To be a self-conscious person, however, is no mere epistemological addendum to receptive consciousness of externals. As conscious of itself this personal awareness reveals itself as having two roots. The first root makes possible (enables) the moral significance of my acts as well as my character. If I can be held responsible for what I do, however, I must assume my moral worth. Thus, worth is not a mere addendum based on the desire to be important, but is rooted in the reality and truth of self-awareness as a person. The second root is that I am worthy beyond the moral—that is, I can be the ground for bestowals, the most surprising and compelling of which is forgiveness. To confront the world so broadly as to include both moral and existential worth demands that I must recognize the non-necessity of my existence and hence of my worth: this recognition is necessarily gratitudinous. Only on the basis of such gratitude is it possible to confront what it means to be in the world as self-reflective. This confrontation is concrete, direct, and real, and hence is fundamental. It is also, by necessity, a confrontation that exceeds complete satisfaction, so it seeks a coherence that is nonschematic—it is thus a species of asking; indeed it is the highest, or most fundamental, asking. Asking, however, whether fundamental or derived, is meaningless without the possibility of some kind of response. The inquiry into the meaning of gratitude is an essential part of that coherence and response.

Reasoning

If it be a mistake to restrict truth solely to answers, leaving questions merely as preveridical stimuli, it may likewise be fallacious to restrict reason only to inferential arguments supporting these answers. The sometime paradigm of reason has often been seen, especially among analytic thinkers, as deductions, conceived as rule-governed inferences from factual assertions in the form of declarative sentences or, on a higher and more dubious level of metaphysical abstraction, in the form of propositions. Under the hegemony of such paradigms, it seems impossible to ascribe reasoning to questioning in any form whatsoever, much less to fundamental asking. Nevertheless, in spite of the fairly hefty endorsement of this paradigm, such restrictive locating of reason must be challenged. It is not enough, however, merely to claim that asking itself can be a form of reasoning. It is necessary to consider what it means to ask such that asking can be a species of reasoning; and what it means to reason such that reasoning can be a species of asking.

To speak of asking as a form of reasoning is not to refer merely to the reasons as motives for why we ask, nor to seek reasons as explanations or justifications of what is asked about, for both of these are extrinsic to the actual asking. What is at question here is how asking itself can be a species of reasoning. In the early chapters of this inquiry, it is already noted that asking—either explicit or implicit—provides coherence, and it is usually accepted that coherence plays a fundamental role in reasoning; but even if this is accepted it is at best vague and imprecise. It is now necessary to discover the greater precision inherent in this suggestion. A few preliminary distinctions must now be made.

Reason is often understood in terms of laws or rules. We must, however, distinguish the use of rules from their discovery, and further, to distinguish their discovery from their legitimacy; and finally to distinguish use, discovery, and legitimacy from the meaning of rules. A student of chemistry may be taught the rule that all chemical reactions must be balanced; and he soon learns from simple instruction how to balance them mathematically—that is by means of more formal rules. Within a short period he learns to balance them with ease, and with this skill he may already be on the way to becoming a very competent, practical chemist in a laboratory. But it takes a more theoretical kind of mind to note that certain chemical phenomena take place because of imbalance, and to discern in such phenomena that the mathematics of equation (balancing) is the explanative reason for the occurrences. When he recognizes how to assign mathematical values to the various elements, we say he has "discovered" the rules or laws governing the behavior of chemical elements. For both the user and the theoretical seeker, rules play a part, but in entirely different ways. In the first we say the practicing chemist uses or applies the rules to account for certain phenomena or even to learn unexpected reactions which can be called discoveries in the experimental sense. The theorist, however, presupposes that there must *be* a "rule," and learns from experimentation or intense mental concentration how to give this as yet hidden "rule" articulation. It is possible, though rather dangerous at this early stage, to suggest that the rule-seeker is asking, whereas the rule-user is answering; but there are perils in this suggestion precisely because the theorist seems also to use further or higher rules in discovering scientific laws. What is thornier is whether the theorist merely uses pre-existing or implicit rules—rules that may be more abstract or simply more general—or whether the asking itself plays a role not accountable by the mere application or assumption of rules. There is the further problem in the suggestion that we may use implicit rules without knowing them explicitly—a point that will be considered in greater detail shortly.

Not all rules suggested by theorists are legitimate, though some may be entertained for a period, used with some success, and then discarded. There are two senses of illegitimacy. The first is that the rule proves unworkable in a sufficient number of cases as to be rejected on pragmatic grounds. The second is that its formal origin is less authoritative than its contender, as when we reject a local government's rule on the basis of inconsistency with the state's constitution, or when a pragmatically successful rule in nature may be discarded and replaced by an equally pragmatic rule which has superior mathematical authority. This nonpragmatic or formal illegitimacy is by far the more disturbing, for the question seems to emerge: Are there higher and lower levels of rules, so that the legitimacy of one kind of rule is based solely on the use of higher rules? Is not the constitution of a state simply a higher set of rules than the local government; is not mathematical authority simply always greater than that of any natural science? How then, do we test the authority of the constitution, or the authority of mathematics?

These last questions suggest the meaning of rules: they are the articulations of manifested or assumed authority. For the user, the rules provide authority, but for the seeker, the authority provides the rules. In order to be used, the authority must be articulated as a rule; but the theorist as seeker does not, strictly speaking, search for the articulated rule. Rather he seeks to articulate what is already manifested as authority. It is perhaps, then, improper to speak of the rule-seeker in the sense there is already a rule that is articulated but somehow yet is hidden. Whether we call them rules, laws, or principles, we speak of them as already articulated—or rather, it is precisely the articulation, either in terms of languages or symbols, that gives access to the authority lurking behind them. It is therefore more precise, and indeed clearer, to deny prediscovered rules, for rules are nothing else but the articulation of authority that in its prearticulated state can be recognized without being identified. It is silly to speak of Newton's laws as pre-existing his formulation of them, for Newton's formulation is precisely what we mean by his laws. To say Newton was looking for Newton's laws would mean he already knew what form they would take, which means he knew the laws before he discovered them. Rather, by the term "discovery" we mean the actual formulation of the authority that had to be presupposed due to the assumed regularity of nature. The preformulated authority is manifested in the emerging coherence of our asking.

A hint as to how this works can be seen in the distinction between implicit and explicit awareness of cohering. Ask a child, "If a tiger and an antelope get in a fight, which animal will win?" and the child will answer "the tiger." How did the child know to shift from the indefinite articles *a* and *an* to the definite article, *the?* Do we say the child implicitly knows the rule governing the usage of definite and indefinite articles? Such rules are extremely complex and subtle; indeed most adults, when challenged to articulate the rule that governs such usage would be hard-pressed. Even professional grammarians disagree on how exactly to formulate this rule. Yet, even a child can use the language properly without even knowing that there are such terms as definite and indefinite articles. The proper usage, as distinguished from improper usages, of the language reveals the authority in its coherence without being articulated. Since the child cannot be said to know the rule as rule, it is misleading to say he "uses" or "applies" the rule, for the child's proper use of the articles is entirely disanalogous to the young chemist's use of the rules governing the balancing of equations. By hearing adults use the language properly, and by being corrected in his misuse, the child learns how to use articles properly. But this propriety is rather an instance of authority rather than rules; and in part this authority is found in the coherence provided by the English language.

It is popular to account for this propriety by speaking of implicit rules; but an "implicit rule" is a highly suspect locution, for when I ask what the "implicit rule" is, a grammarian states it in its explicit form. It seems legitimate to admit there may be vague or inexact rules that are used successfully; but in such cases the user knows there is a rule and that he is applying it—but it is not at all obvious that the child's proper use of English articles entails an awareness of using even a vague rule. Rather the authority in the grammatical coherence of the English language is learned directly *as* authoritative, and only because of this can there be "rules" of grammar at all. Are we not, however, in danger of simply replacing one troubling term, *rule*, with another, *authority*? Both terms may indeed be troubling to some extent, but they are still *different;* and we can note this difference, and on the basis of it decide which is prior. To say the child learns the English language as authoritative is to say simply that by being corrected in his misusage he learns there is a proper and an improper way to speak—there is no sense at all of rules being applied; but there is a sense that speaking can be proper and improper, and that the propriety matters. That this propriety later on can be schematized into rules merely shows that the authority inherent in the difference between the proper and the improper is the basis for the rules. This suggests that it is authority that is the basis for the rules, at least on the original or fundamental level. In the case of the junior chemist it was noted, however, that in certain specialized cases, the rule can be the basis of authority; but we now can see that this usage of rules as authoritative is derived or nonfundamental.

If we suggest that to reason is to think with authority, and add that authority is the basis of all rules, then we cannot define reason solely in terms of following or even seeking rules, either explicit or implicit. Authority can now be suggested to be that mode or aspect of thinking which, in achieving coherence, enables nonarbitrary understanding. Rules are simply the formal articulations of how this enabling sometimes occurs, and are always subsequent to authority formally or fundamentally, but which, as used, can provide further or derived authority to specific, controlled endeavors. This distinction between authority derived from rules and rules derived from authority can now be applied to questioning and asking. In ordinary questioning the scheme of coherence which gives such questioning rational authority is presupposed as a rule or as if it were a rule. Thus, to ask what time it is appeals to the already established scheme of the twenty-four-hour day—the questioner does not establish or discover this convention, he uses it. His question, though, still brings authority to how a given answer is possible, and hence can be seen as a species of reasoning. Asking, however does not simply use a scheme but seeks either to articulate a scheme, or even, in fundamental asking, to seek the originary coherence, and hence authority. The rule-seeker as asker, thus is more rational than the rule-user, either as answerer, or as questioner using schemes.

The distinction between authority and rules, however, has greater significance than the mere question of priority. For if authority is prior to rules, it must now be asked whether all authority is able to be articulated in rules, or whether rational authority is sometimes found entirely independent of rules altogether. It is impossible to ask this question without first distinguishing, as we have done, between rules and authority; but with the distinction this new question becomes crucial, because if authority can be without rules it is much easier to see how fundamental asking itself can be a species of reasoning.

Before turning to what it means to reason without employing or entailing rules, however, it is necessary first to see how authority as the basis of rules throws light on certain classical problems inherent in thinking as if rules provide authority on the fundamental level—which they cannot do. It is because rules can provide authority on nonfundamental levels of asking that leads us to this error: an understandable error, perhaps, but all the more insidious for its seeming legitimacy.

From the very beginning of critical philosophy a recognized problem has emerged as having special status: What are the ultimate principles of thought, and how do these principles tell us, if at all, anything about reality? There is already a danger here: Why do we use the term *principle?* Apparently *principle* is an a priori law or rule which governs how we think—or how we ought to think if we are to think successfully. This suggestion, however, puts us not in a critical mode but in a skeptical mode; for there are now two insurmountable—and ultimately artificial or at least unnecessary—problems. The first is How do we recognize that we have ever arrived at fundamental principles? Consider, for example, that Aristotle gives *reasons* for accepting the principle of noncontradiction. Are these reasons even more fundamental than what is being explained? Surely not. But it is the second question that reveals the skeptical superstition inherent in this sublime instance of bad questioning. How can we know, we ask, how or whether these "principles" of thought correspond to what is real? Before we even try to answer this, consider what we are being asked to do. What principles do I use—or even what considerations can I possibly make?—that would answer this question without begging it? The very formulation of the question has put the "world" or "reality" beyond the unscalable walls of artificial ignorance. Given this formulation the question simply cannot be answered since it demands a godlike third perspective, neither mind nor world but somehow including them. Once we recognize—as most great philosophers do and lesser philosophers don't— that principles are the articulations of inherently recognizable authority, the hopelessness of the problem is overcome. There is still a problem—indeed a fundamental and hence a great problem—but no longer a silly one. Principles are not ultimate, but the authority that is articulated by the principle is fundamental—and to some extent, available. There are good reasons to celebrate those whose critical powers enable them to codify recognized authority, thereby providing us with principles or rules; but it is hagiographic illusion to rank the principle as the source of the authority, giving such thinkers miraculous powers they would be ashamed to accept. To conceive principles so sacrosanctically is akin to equating the reflective thinker to the gunman whose raw appeal to power rather than authority enforces his will on those he terrorizes; or perhaps a better simile would be that the formulator of principles is akin to the divine author of a sacred text that is believed simply because it comes from that author. Even on the human level we do not accept the principle of sufficient reason simply because a wise man named Leibniz is so smart we must believe what he says. It is surely the other way around, showing once more that authority precedes principle, at least on the fundamental level. Thus Aristotle is quite right to argue for the principle of noncontradiction, for his arguments are meant to reveal the authority that gives rise to the articulation of the principle.

There is another preliminary danger. Many epistemologists, quite legitimately, speak of reason-giving; but some quite illegitimately use this terminology as the sole access to understanding the nature of reasoning itself. A remark should be made at this point: strictly speaking, the capital form of the term should be *reasoning* and not *reason*, for the latter term means either a faculty (as Kant uses it) or a specific instance of a supportive account that depends on what is supported for its intelligibility. If I "give a reason" for my action, the action is conceived as an independent thing which then is supported or justified by externalist props that can be "given"—which seems to suggest they could also be withheld. I am prompted to support my action only when there is a challenge. Merely to provide a motive is not enough; I must somehow show that the motive is one which would be endorsed by any thinking person because it is based on a universal law or principle. The danger here, though not inevitable, is great—that I begin to think of "reasons" as isolated building blocks in propositional form that function solely as *supportive;* also, that these supports are supports only insofar as they are "given." But what is it that I "give"? To say I give reasons is to put the verbal emphasis on the giving not on the reasoning. The image created here is that of a whole host of possible accounts, some of which are flagged as acceptable reasons, others as unacceptable accounts because they are wanton or whimsical, hence not "reasons." This procedure overlooks the phenomenological basis of reasoning as authoritative thinking. The "giving" of reason is not the same as the reasoning of reasons. Where is the thinking in such a model? Is the thinking an earlier event that went on prior to allowing me to tag some accounts as reasons and others as not? But this disjoins reasoning from *the* reasons. Or is the reasoning contained in the *giving?* But I also can "give" nonreasoned accounts. There is much danger in speaking of reasoning made up of a plurality of reasons. It is the other way around. It is reasoning that gives us reasons.

If it is reasoning that gives us reasons, then we can see the significance of this warning in terms of the central question. How is asking a species of reasoning—and not merely a species of reason-giving.

If coherence achieves unity, then it is when that unity is conceived as authoritative that we have what is called universality. Universality, as nonarbitrary, in obviously the point in articulating rules, or even in making laws—which, as laws, govern all equally unless particularity is part of the law itself. But there are ways of achieving universality that are not at all dependent on being able to be articulated by rules, as when we recognize the universality of a truth revealed in an artwork or embodied in a paradigm or prototype.

If the artwork is not verbal, its independence from possible articulation into rules is clearer. The surging triumph within the musical conflict and emergence in Beethoven's *Eroica* symphony can be said to reveal universal truth about all human beings, a truth heard only in the actual music and not discoverable by the mere reading of interpreters' analyses in the program notes or on the CD packet. In writing the *Eroica* Beethoven obviously made use of musicological rules; but it is not his use of these rules, nor our recognition of them that elevates the work to the level of a truth-revealing masterpiece. Nor is it the case that even the most profound musicological account of the *Eroica* can in any way suffice or be substituted for the actual hearing of the symphony; and this means that the universality within the piece itself cannot be articulated as rules. Yet that there is universality in the *Eroica* can be denied only at the dreadful cost of stubbornist folly. Does this, then, suggest that, in the case of artworks, there is universality achieved entirely independently of reasoning? This suggestion seems far too high a price to pay, especially since a more amenable suggestion is readily at hand. There is nothing to prohibit us from suggesting that the universality in the *Eroica* is learned by means of what might be called rational hearing, or hearing as a way of reasoning. Just as we can hear the authority in a well-constructed deductive argument, so we can hear the authority in great music. The former can be articulated into rules, the latter cannot, but in both cases, the universality is achieved by rational hearing.

If this suggestion is a coherent one, it would then seem that by analogy it is possible to suggest that fundamental asking also provides authority independent of rule-articulation. There is no doubt that even rule-articulated authority can be discovered between questions, as for example when asking whether fruit trees grow well in sandy soil entails asking whether pear trees grow well in sandy soil. Merely because these are questions in no way bars the efficacy of the rules of entailment—though in spite of this obvious counter-example some purists continue to insist that the rules of logic operate only between propositions. It is not the efficacy of the rules of entailment, however, that accounts for the suggestion that asking is itself able to provide rational authority without rules. If the analogy to music is to hold we must consider whether certain ways of asking provide authority in its universalizing, as the *Eroica*, merely as music, universalizes something about our humanity. There is a danger in relying too much on the universality of the *topic*, whether revealed in music or in asking. One might argue, for example, that the truths concerning human courage are first known prior to and independently of our hearing the *Eroica*, and the actual phenomenon of hearing the symphony merely moves us emotionally to remember or reflect upon nonmusically derived truth. Hence there would be no such thing as rational hearing of music, and therefore no analogic support for rational asking. The universality exists solely in how we think about such things as courage, and either the artwork or the asking merely prods us to recollect or instantiate the earlier learned reasoning. This objection however is phenomenologically unsound, for our appreciation of great art or even great asking is not a mere mnemonic device. Furthermore, the question is not whether there might be other ways of reasoning which produce *similar* access to universality, but whether what happens in our rational hearing of great art and our rational hearing of great asking is authoritative in a way that is fundamentally *dissimilar* to rule-governed forms of authoritative thinking. In other words, the question is not about the universality of the topic, but about the universalizing inherent in certain special ways of hearing that can be called rational hearing.

How do we hear with authority? Listening to the *Eroica* in such a way as to submit to its authority in revealing something about our own humanity is obviously one example. Hearing our own internal indictment of ourselves in the case of guilt, and submitting to its authority is another. The censure brought against me as being guilty is authoritative—that is, I cannot, without deep self-deception, escape the legitimacy of the censure that isolates me, and so I must submit to it; and this reveals my own unique enabling grounded in the possibility within my actuality. It is not at all obvious that this self-censuring and self-submitting inherent in being guilty is based on rules—the submissive hearing of my self-censure is something I do, it has authority, it reveals something fundamental and nonreducible about myself and yet, as authoritative it nevertheless universalizes; but there are no rules that account for my guilt nor is the submissive hearing of my own indictment at all similar to the young chemist following—hearing and obeying the authority in—the rules of science, nor is it similar to the theorist who hears the authority in his own thinking about nature so as to articulate it in terms of rules. Since I alone bear the responsibility for being guilty, there can be no generalization—which *may* require rules—but there is universality just because there is inescapable authority. What can be universalized is the enabling of being guilty.

These two examples, hearing the *Eroica*, and hearing my own indictment of myself in guilt indicate that hearing itself can be rational just because it can be authoritative, and as authoritative it is a species of coherence that universalizes. In both cases there is authority without the use of or appeal to rules. In the same way, asking can be authoritative in its universality precisely when, like guilt, it universalizes ourselves; or, like hearing the *Eroica*, it reveals universal truth about ourselves. This is what happens when, for example, we participate as thinkers in hearing (reading) a Platonic dialogue. Indeed, the aporetic dialogues may even be seen as showing that we can and do discuss the virtues without the rules—the precise definitions—which, when articulated as rules, always collapse. The very fact that the interlocutors of the aporetic dialogues learn that various suggestions about the definition fail shows that the authority inherent in the inquiry is independent of any precise definition, particularly when a definition is used as a rule. This realization may show more than that this particular definition is inadequate, but that any definition at all must be inadequate. We learn this by rationally hearing the dialogue unfold as authoritative.

Various points can now be made if we assume that rational hearing is based upon the authority inherent in asking. The first, and perhaps most basic, is that we recognize there can be both good and bad asking. We can ask whether we are asking well. We can also ask whether certain ways of asking are helpful—indeed even legitimate—but not yet fundamental. This ability to ask about asking is crucial, for it shows there is authority in asking about asking, hence—and this is the second point—there is authority in asking, available only in asking. The third point is that this authority does not reside solely in the raising or posing of questions, but in hearing the authority in the actual ongoing phenomenon of inquiry. The fourth point is that the authority in asking heard by rational hearing rests in part on the continuing of coherence that is inherent in extended inquiry: I always can ask deeper and deeper questions—an enablement that assures the continuing critique, and with this the respect I have for the ability to ask further questions and to discern when these questions are trivial and when they open up further reaching by the authority of asking. However, it is the fifth and final point that distinguishes all other asking from fundamental asking: since only fundamental asking always must include asking about asking, we discover that fundamental asking is both reflective and reflexive. It is reflective because such asking must always include our own asking; and it is reflexive because this asking changes not only our understanding of who we are but our own being who we are. We are fundamentally changed by asking fundamentally.

It is reflexivity and reflectivity that give to fundamental asking its unique and originary authority. There can be no further or externalist authority that accounts for what is both reflexive and reflective. Since all assertive claims have been shown to rely at least indirectly on the preassertive coherence provided by either explicit or implicit questioning, such reflexive-reflective authority must always be found only in the asking, and not in the answering. The suggestion that authoritative thinking is what is meant by reasoning now reveals that not only is asking a species of reasoning but that fundamental asking—that is, asking that is both reflective and reflexive—is fundamental reasoning, and hence is the highest species of reasoning.

These five discoveries are within the range of what is called rational hearing. However, we now realize that such hearing must precede the raising or posing of specific questions. I first hear the question as emerging authority before I can articulate it in specific form. Thus it is not necessarily someone else who first raises the question which I then hear—though this may occur—but rather the asker as asker first hears the authority in reflective and reflexive thinking. This accounts for the insistence that no single question—however profound—is always and ever the only way of formulating fundamental asking. What then is the origin of that authoritative call or sound that we hear? Since fundamental rational hearing as asking is reflective-reflexive, the hearing itself is the call; or, to be more precise, it is the enabling of hearing that is the call. There is no need to seek externalist sources for what is heard. Indeed, if rational hearing can be reflexive and reflective, such externalist sources would be impossible. There must, however, be something about the very nature of the enablement that enables rational hearing that belongs to our own being, if such enablement is to be made available. This enablement has already been seen in the existential analyses that precede this chapter. The suggestion is now possible: gratitude enables reflectivity; irony enables reflexivity.

Gratitude has been shown to rely on the fact of a contingent existence aware of its own contingency; irony has been shown to be a figure of reflexivity: as the contingent existent unfolds itself as a story, the nature of that unfolding enables its own being affected by the story. As a figure of speech, irony enables the story to constitute a necessary part of the coherence that makes thinking about a fated (contingent) story thinkable. The ability to recognize that irony provides authority in the telling of stories enables the hearer to appreciate what it means to be revealed in an asking that is reflexive. To protest that irony is only an aesthetic device, or that not all stories are ironic is to miss the point. Fundamental asking reveals itself ironically, that is: we ask, expecting an answer, and there is indeed an answer, but only in the form of a deeper question. Rather than depressing us, such realization of the irony of fundamental asking constitutes another irony: that we can take joy in this discovery even as it frustrates.

There is a final point to be made concerning the rational priority of asking. There is something dead about the terminating closure of an answer and something vital or alive about the eager probing that is asking. "And they lived happily ever after" puts an end to all the thrilling adventures we heard in our youth; the story was about the struggle or the journey or the solving. When the young prince saves the princess there is no more to tell; no child wants to hear of the fairly dull married life that follows the glorious wedding, and no storyteller would dare to include such mundane matters for fear of losing his audience, or worse, revealing how banal the prince and princess truly were. The vitality of asking seems to be the very spark that ignites the fire of inquiry. To be sure, answers do play a role, but curiously they seem to serve as bridges between levels of asking, rather than, as is normally seen, the asking providing the bridges between answers. There is something of a paradox in this, since after all we really do ask in order to learn, which seems to place the achievement of such wisdom as the ultimate goal, and hence its ultimate justification. Yet it is also obvious that reasoning itself serves our inquiry; it hardly serves the contented as answered. Why reason at all if we already know—if the asked is already answered?

What this seems to suggest is that reasoning is not merely a way of testing whether our answers are correct, nor is it merely problem-solving, unless that "problem" just be our finitude, which, ironically can never be "finished" or answered. Rather, reasoning as asking is a species of daring—a probing into darkness that lures us just because it is our own darkness, but which nonetheless, as darkness, imperils. The peril is genuine—indeed asking badly may be more perilous than answering badly; but facing perils is the essence of adventure, and only the boldly adventurous can be said to live life to the fullest. What must be grasped here is that the power which enables this boldness—perhaps even hubris—is inherent in the awe and sublimity in a fundamental confrontation found only in the ability to ask. David usurps a privilege in assuming an intimacy for which he has no legitimate claim—the privilege to demand of God explanations of what he cannot understand—a species of lèse-majesté that is, apparently, overlooked by graciousness. This daring is a way of reasoning, because, as asking it *establishes* an authority unavailable to the nondaring. Even though this establishment may well be usurpatory in the sense that it is not sanctioned, it is nevertheless given a kind of legitimacy solely on the basis of its boldness. The audacious in battle often secure a victory, and hence an authority, beyond their resources. To ask fundamentally perhaps always must be audacious in some sense—that is, in reaching beyond itself it enables itself in a new way, even as it imperils. There is no peril in death, only life has perils; there is a safety in answers that is nonperilous. To reason is to think with authority; but in fundamental asking this authority is audacious, a thrust of life itself into reaches beyond itself simply because it is about itself.

The recognition that reasoning is asking helps to avoid the excesses that find in reasoning an avenue for achieving perfect knowledge. It may strike us as pathetically comic to learn what this hagiography of reason actually achieved during the Enlightenment. The great philosopher Leibniz apparently was anxious lest his physician friends not discover more quickly the ultimate nostrum against all human disease, and hence the possibility of an endless life here on earth. He thought it an outrage that he, the most deserving, would die before these discoveries—which he was fairly certain would actually occur—were made. This sounds silly to the contemporary ear, more jaded now with the false promise of reason as the true tyrant of the soul. The deification of reason during the French Revolution, or even the later deification of the inevitable dialectic espoused by Marxists, seem to mock rather than revere what may still be a noble faculty. The Lisbon earthquake of 1755 shook all Europe by its death toll surpassing thirty thousand people; they simply could not grasp that any such thing could happen in an age of Reason—and many non-Portuguese committed suicide because of this assault on what was "reasonable." This was a superstition—a naive misapprehension of what reason is capable of. As a superstition we might call it the irrationality of the rational. If today we see these superstitions merely as naive, however, we are apt to overlook similar tendencies in our own putative enlightenment, based now on "science" rather than reason, and supported by the mushrooming of first the industrial and then the technological revolutions. Kant's critique of—or asking about—reason showed us its limits; but in his antinomic dialectic he also showed us the boldness inherent in rational asking. That there is profound irony in these historic reflections reveals that irony itself is a part of self-reflexive (and self-reflective) reasoning. It is only because we reason about reasoning that we can see its limits; but it is also only by the boldness of innovative asking that we enliven what otherwise is moribund. Were we to discover all the laws of nature, would we then no longer need to reason, or even be able to reason? The very fact that we can ask this question seriously shows us that reason, ironically, is both more limited than we may have thought, but also more open to wider ranges than we now think. Our asking reveals ourselves as askers, and since this truth is authoritative, it is a species of reasoning. The model of reasoning as structured or coherently interrelated answers must fall away before the onslaught of this bold asking; for life is more authoritative than death, even though the latter seems the final victor. It cannot be the final victor since in life we can think about death but the dead do not think about life. As reasoners, asking about our own asking with authority is our essence.

10

Seven Questions

Throughout this inquiry emphasis has been placed on what it means to ask fundamentally, and hence to avoid focusing on a traditional list of "the" great questions. There can be no final or ultimate list, since such a list would limit beforehand our ability to ask why this list and no other. Nevertheless, it is myopic and disingenuous to deny that in our history certain specific questions have been asked that not only had enormous influence on subsequent thinking, but even today are still powerful enough—if we truly *ask* them again—to reveal the fundamental nature of asking. Some of these questions deserve to be considered as remarkable achievements or even as paradigms of the ability to reason in the mode of asking.

Consider the sheer power of these following questions if they are genuinely asked—and what it means to ask them at all, without leaping immediately to our favorite answers.

Is virtue teachable?
Why is there evil; why is there good?
What cannot be doubted?
How is geometry possible?

Why are there things rather than nothing?
Am I a coward? Who calls me villain?
Who told thee thou wert naked?

The askers of these seven questions can be named in the order they are listed: Plato, Augustine, Descartes, Kant, Heidegger, Hamlet, Genesis. Though the first five were asked by philosophers, the questions have an independence of any specific discipline: they seem to echo the universality of the whole species as the asking spirit; there are more, of course: this is but a selection. It should be noted that none of them is the conventional favorite of the text books. There are no questions about whether God exists or how to define anything or what the ultimate stuff of the universe may be. They ask in a slightly shocking way; yet in raising them as questions, they can and do penetrate into the very essence of the asking mystery. A brief sketch of each is here offered to show how they enable fundamental asking.

To ask if virtue is teachable, stuns. We find ourselves already in a culture; we see the efforts of teachers to instruct the young; yet we see some who have been taught who are yet wicked. Have we failed as teachers? The unexamined assumption that virtue is teachable is very deep, for why else do we correct children in improper behavior, or threaten adults with punishment, or, perhaps more disturbing: Why do we fear lest our children be indoctrinated into cults, hate groups, racist political parties, or decadent sects, unless we know bad education *is* possible? The grim fact remains: not all—perhaps not even ourselves in some secret part of us—are rendered virtuous by our cultural devices. Both possible answers, yes and no, seem almost to distract by their eclipse of the agony. This is not a definitionalist enterprise, as if tinkering with the accounts of virtue and teaching would ever remove the terrible onslaught of what this asking confronts. It is this asking, and not the questions of the definitions, that reveals fundamentally, both as reflective and reflexive. There is dread irony in the realization that good men have bad sons; and this irony bids us to reflect, accepting perforce the reality of fate; yet as it bids it also forbids: cruelly, the irony does not relieve us of the burden to continue teaching. Perhaps it is like the doomed sailor in the leaking lifeboat—he bails furiously to the very end, even as he knows it is bootless, for what would it mean to stop bailing?

It is perhaps a refinement to ask not whether good fathers have bad sons but whether good teachers have bad students—lest we shrug off the confrontation by saying the good father was simply a bad teacher. Yet even this tinkering seems almost effete, for it is part of what we mean by a good father that he import his goodness to his son; and if this transmission across the generations somehow fails—what does this mean? Is not all good teaching in part a teaching about teaching? It may seem that the question of whether virtues are merely custom or part of reality is the worthier formulation; but that way of asking amuses the sophist more than it addresses the fundamental torment. We ask if virtue is teachable not as externalist nonteachers amused by the paradox, but as inevitable teachers, doomed to teach regardless of our unsuccess, wondering what it means. Do we really mean to suggest that the wicked are wicked simply because they are untaught? Perhaps we do mean this if by teaching we mean only successful teaching; and this becomes even more acceptable if we recognize that true teaching is not mere instruction, but letting learning happen, which further means that the student himself is in part a self-teacher. If this seems to ease the shame of a good father with a bad son, however, we must wonder whether these reflections are becoming answers that somehow have lost contact with their origin in asking. Teaching cannot be merely successful teaching, for then there could be no bad teachers, but bad teachers are precisely those whom we rightly fear. And even if we recognize the learner is part of the equation, since the learner is our son, his nonlearning still indicts us in some way. The problem then is not that we do not know what teaching and virtue are; the problem is that we *do* know—at least we know enough to see how fundamental this asking is. If we deem ourselves virtuous at all, then we must have had good teachers, and for this we must be grateful—for the suggestion makes it imperative that existing nonvirtuously is possible. So the reflectivity of gratitude for being taught links up with the ironic reflexivity of the burden of teaching even though we are not all-wise.

What enables us to learn? What enables us to be virtuous? Are they the same? Coming to grips with the finitude of our knowledge requires more than the mere possession of that knowledge; the very knowledge we have reveals our limits as learners. What enables us to learn is then not some extra-epistemic quality such as curiosity, but simply the limit built into our already knowing and the need to confront that limit. In the same way, the enabling of virtue does not reside either in the mere assimilation of a culture's sanctions and taboos or in our critical powers to figure out how to invent new ones, but in the dread realization of our moral limit. To ask if virtue can be taught is thus to confront ourselves as knowingly limited in our knowledge and virtuously limited in our virtue. The greatest dread is that virtue cannot be taught, for then our virtuous learning of learning virtue deceives; and we denude ourselves as ultimately impotent. Since we can and do ask, however, this denuding is itself a learning of our own enablement, and therein lies the ironic splendor that truth matters fundamentally, even if we lack knowledge. To ask if virtue can be taught thus enables our confrontation with what is fundamental.

This asking reveals that seeking precise definitions, though important, cannot be fundamental, but asking about being able to teach, to learn, and to be virtuous, is.

The danger is, we may lose it entirely—this sense of the reality of evil; and as a consequence, the reality of good.

The four-year-old was caught in the sudden sweep of fire across the arid fields; severely burned, she howled in fierce anguish for six interminable days before death wrenched her small, blackened frame, leaving behind only the heavy pall of bitter grief. The wind, the lightning that sparked the fire, the shape of the hills that funneled the conflagration down into her valley, the nerve endings in her body, the vulnerability of human flesh to intense heat— all these are natural phenomena. They happen. Each of them, as events, are explicable only in terms of causes; their untimely coalescence, however, is simply coincidence—which means it cannot be thought about purposively or in terms of broader meaning. What about our grief, our sadness, perhaps even our outrage? They, too are natural phenomena; though each has its cause, they just happen. The mother's eclipsing affliction is also explained by nerve endings functioning as they always do. What would it mean to curse our neural synapses or the wind? Even the cursing is itself but a neurological response to stimuli. We know that cursing the wind or the hot, dry summer or the lightning, changes none of them; they are impervious to our howls. We are left bereft of any explanation, left only with the pain, which, in time will ease, or cease altogether with our death. We may call her death an evil thing, but if we mean by evil simply that she suffered, or that we, contemplating it, have our own torment, then perhaps the most prudent thing is to cease thinking about it at all, since strictly speaking it cannot be *thought* about, just accepted as a fact.

There are some who would persuade us that, in the light of things beyond our ken, there is a justifying purpose, perhaps a personal God arranging things for the best, with the caveat that the best is not understandable by mortal means. We then say her suffering was not evil, but, since all is good, so is her anguish. Even if this were so we cannot, by the very premises given, understand it. She suffered, and contemplating it, we still suffer. The only difference is we now call it good rather than evil. The naturalist is really akin to the theodicist, here; they both reduce what we call evil to something more fundamental, beyond our ken, where the word *evil* does not belong. God and natural coincidence are both inexplicable, unthinkable, and most importantly, unjudgeable. It does not take us long to reach this impasse, whichever route we take. Under both accounts, evil soon vanishes entirely.

There is irony in this. The naturalist accuses the theodicist of sanitizing evil (pain) by appealing to metaphysics; the theodicist accuses the naturalist of sanitizing evil by appealing to metaphysics (there is only nature); so both despise the other because evil is denied, and both putative denials are grounded in metaphysics. Perhaps there is some wisdom here: metaphysics is the mistake; metaphysics is evil because the most evil thing is its denial. Yet, the hurtful ache cannot be so glibly dismissed. We may not be very good at metaphysics, but questions about evil always turn on questions about the reality of evil, and thus the metaphysical cannot be shunned merely because bad metaphysics is so easy.

Earlier in the inquiry it was suggested that ordinary questions rely on imagined schemes to give coherence, whereas fundamental asking is rooted in the reality of our own coherence seen as possibility within our own actuality. Appeals to a naturalist, mechanistic metaphysics use a very successful imagined scheme in order to question coherently. Appeals to an ultimate machine of divine dimensions dispensing, by nature of its inherent goodness, only good things is also a very successful imagined scheme, providing coherence. We are considering here, not an answer to the problems of evil, but the asking of them, and whether such asking is fundamental. Imagined schemes providing structures of coherence must always reveal their limits, and thereby provide only provisional coherence. If we ask about the meaning of evil in terms of our own enablement, we find that evil is precisely that which disables, not the fact, but the possibility of being our own reality as persons. Whatever else evil might mean, before it even can become a question, much less a problem, it eclipses the possibility of being a person. Naturalist metaphysics, especially as mechanistic, accounts for persons by reducing them to machines, thereby denying their nonreducible reality. Theodicists account for persons by reducing them to products of, and purposes for, a superior kind of being. To ask fundamentally is to raise our asking on the basis of our own enabling coherence as self-reflective and self-reflexive thinkers—persons.

Is this not, however, slipping into a species of answering? The suggestion that evil is a disabling of the possibility of being a person seems very much a definition of sorts, and thus an answer. In truth, however, this suggestion is merely a refinement of fundamental asking. It tells us what it means to ask about evil: namely, that the term itself is meaningless except as a seeking of coherence in our own possibility. To be sure, as providing coherence, it establishes what counts and matters, as the question about the time excludes answers that are entirely nontemporal. The critique of two possible answers, naturalism and theodicy, reveals something about what the asking about evil means, but it does not thereby answer it.

Why do we ask about evil and not about good? Is there any compelling reason why our own happiness should somehow be required or necessary; or that goodness is somehow unproblematic, and only evil deserves thought? There certainly are reasons for doing what is morally right, so that I can quite legitimately say I ought to do those acts that I ought to do. If by *good* we mean being moral, there is no problem at all with evil in the sense of undeserved suffering; for whether I suffer or not I still ought to be moral. This merely shows that the word *good* has variant meanings. Perhaps evil is also a moral, and not a natural, property. The death of the child by naturally ignited brush fires would then be unfortunate, but not evil since evil requires censure. Perhaps so, but even if it were true—which is dubious—this would not let the theodicist off the hook; whatever we call it we still need to make sense of a world in which undeserved and unanswered wrongs do in fact occur; but in this same world human reasoning is expected to account for all things. What does not seem obvious, however, is that reason demands we all be maximally happy—as delightful, or possibly boring, as this may be. Even this questioning, however, forces us beyond the limits of ordinary thinking.

What would it mean *not* to ask about why there is evil or even why there is good? Such insouciance itself seems to indict. Indict of what? Words such as *insensitive* or *callous* or even *nihilistic* may come to mind, but none of these is enough. To confront what it means to be able to be evil and to be able to be good seems a necessary part of our humanity. The perpetrators of horrors, those agents of evil who blot the chronicles of our common story, are in some ways less outrageous than those who are so hugely indifferent that they suspend judgment even of the most wicked, a judgment which the wicked themselves need not suspend. There seems a certain irreducibility about being a person, the denial of which, whether by metaphysics, intense prejudice, or religious zealotry, so profoundly confounds our thinking that we are forced by its occurrence to ask beyond the entertainment of imagined schemes. There must be more to us that can be asked than that which merely assumes such a scheme. To ask what it means for there to be evil and good confronts our own reality, and this reality itself alone can provide the nonschematic coherence that is ultimate or fundamental.

From this asking we rediscover concretely the nonreducibility of the asker.

Doubting matters. Because it matters, the asking enables the distinction between doubting wisely and doubting unwisely. Descartes's great asking is far superior to his response to it; doubting cannot be an algorithm or even a method in the thematic sense. What enables doubting? The first key is the fundamentality of modal reasoning: we are directly aware of the differences between possibility, actuality, impossibility, and necessity. Asking about doubting forces us to be aware of these differences—perhaps we may even say it *necessitates* this awareness, which is already subtly ironic, even droll. How is it possible for contingent beings like ourselves even to be aware of such a thing as necessity? Once we realize that being aware of our contingency already entails the possibility of the noncontingent—either the impossible or the necessary—the question becomes not less but more troubling, for I am not contingently aware of my contingency but necessarily aware of it, but only as long as I think about it. It is not, however, necessary that I do think about it—most of us do not reflect on such matters for weeks at a time—and hence my necessarily being aware of my contingency is itself contingent. How, then, can I say I am necessarily aware of my contingency if such awareness is itself contingent? This bemused slogging through the treacle of modal logic is redeemable precisely because it is both silly and profound. It is silly because we are creating false problems—doubting badly—but it is profound because the realization of what makes them false is of great significance, a realization that is the result of doubting well.

It is an astonishing peculiarity of modal logic that the denial of mere possibility enables a necessary judgment; for when I deny that x is possible I am saying necessarily there is no x; and this shift from what seems the weakest of all claims (it is logically possible that x) to the strongest of all claims (it is necessarily the case that non-x), seems usurpatory. Yet, the logic does not fail us here: what seems to escape us is how it is possible to think this way and what it means. To ask what cannot be doubted apparently is to ask what must be. We cannot escape the burden of this asking—we know what it means to doubt, and since doubting is a meaningful thing to do, we also must know what not doubting, trusting, means. But can we truly be said to *know* what cannot be doubted? I do not really doubt that summer

will follow spring; but I can entertain fantastic possibilities in which summer does not follow spring. This suggests that actual doubting and being
able to doubt are quite different. To ask if there is something that cannot be
doubted seems thus to ask for a mere possibility, not an actuality. But if it
turns out to be actual, then, being undoubtable, it would be necessary.
However, to reflect on my actual doubting is quite another thing than to ask
about my possible doubting—that I can do the one does not entail I can do
the other. It seems, at first glance, that modal logic abets us here: whatever
is must also be possible. Thus to doubt entails being able to doubt; but curiously not doubting does not entail being unable to doubt. Furthermore,
being contingent is not the same as knowing contingently. The fact of noncontingent knowledge, such as $2 + 4 = 6$, in no way affirms any noncontingent *thing*. This is often designated as the de-re/de-dicto distinction. Thus,
it would seem I do know with absolute certainty something—$2 + 4 = 6$—
and therefore cannot doubt it. Yet . . . ?

Is this really true? It is clear I *do not* doubt that $2 + 4 = 6$, but is it necessary to say I *cannot* doubt it? There may be as yet undiscovered truths that
are certain. To suggest this is to say truths can be certain without being certainly known. This reveals a subtle ambiguity: on the one hand *certain* can
refer to having a specific state of mind: I am certain he will call before noon.
On the other hand, *certain* can designate a specific quality about a claim: it
is certain that if you halve an odd whole number the result will be two non-
whole halves. Many nonmathematical types may not be certain of this at all,
but it is still a certain—necessary—claim. Perhaps then, quite seriously, we
cannot ask what cannot be doubted, but only what we do not doubt.

We are doubting and trusting beings. The originality and fundamentality of asking about the limits of each is revealing. Neither trusting nor
doubting is ever absolute, for if I *know* something or someone will fail me
I cannot doubt, for doubting always entails the possibility that what is
doubted could be true. If I know with certainty the loyalty of my friend
neither can I then trust him, for trust implies some sense of possible
betrayal: I do not trust that $2 + 7 = 9$, and consequently then, neither can
I doubt it. There may be, then, a fatal shift in seeking to establish certainty
on the basis of something which is a value precisely because it is uncer-
tain—as trusting and doubting obviously are. Yet this in no way forfeits the
fundamentality of Descartes's asking, for being both trusting and doubting are
essential for our being finite thinkers. We are also both knowing and ignorant.
What is of crucial significance is that these pairs are entirely distinct and non-
interchangeable. In this precise sense, Descartes's question is too easily

answered: I cannot doubt whatever I know; but I cannot trust what I know either. It is not his question but his asking that matters; and for the asker doubting and trusting are more fundamental than knowing and ignorance.

If, as this inquiry suggests, irony can reflect the reflexivity of fundamental asking, it is both ironic and even droll to point out something about Descartes. For all his fame as a skeptic, and bearing in mind that he insists he doubts, or tries to doubt, everything, there is nothing more ironic than Descartes's absolute trust in his method. Consider what he tells us: by following this method he is already sure that the ensuing results will produce absolute certainty and truth; he assures us of this even before he puts his method into practice. Many arrogant thinkers claim they have solved all the great problems—a bit of hubris that may even be necessary for the boldness of true inquiry—but at least they have the decency to wait until after they have worked through their analysis. Descartes, though, tells us he knows in advance, even before we see a single claim or argument, that the method is foolproof. Talk about trust! Descartes is the most trusting thinker who ever wrote.

Doubting and trusting are both phenomena which unlike knowing and being ignorant can be done either well or badly. To trust badly is a species of naivete, that, when applied to epistemic procedures, amounts to a lack of critique sufficiently severe as to be irrational. We do possess critical powers, and if we fail to use them properly, we become vulnerable to superstition and indefensible suggestions. To doubt badly, however, is also possible. When a juror stubbornly insists that, in spite of the overwhelming evidence, he entertains purely logical doubts based on fantastic speculation, he is engaged in unreasonable doubting. There are, however, more subtle forms of bad doubting; as when one doubts another's motives solely on the basis of personal animosity, a species of what Sartre calls *mauvais foi*. I can doubt the motives of an otherwise trustful person beyond any acceptable reason; indeed I can generalize this falsely as an exercise in normative critique and doubt that any motive is other than what a speculative reductionist offers. Thus to doubt that one can act unselfishly, even in the face of one's own personal experience in acting for the sake of another, is to doubt solely for the sake of supporting a dubious reductionism of motives, such as that which claims all motives are based on the pleasure principle. It is thus clear that both doubting and trusting can be either rational or irrational, precisely because of their limits. It is pushing beyond those limits that leads Descartes to suggest that, though rational and irrational doubting and trusting occur in specific contexts, when taken to epistemic extremes, they provide a method for discerning truth. This use of extremity forces doubting and trusting beyond the meaning, not merely in the sense of one's psychological incapacity, but in the precise sense of what the two phenomena actually mean.

These reflections now reveal the second key to the fundamentality of this asking. What enables doubting? The answer is that we are both knowing and ignorant: I can neither trust nor doubt if I know nothing; but neither can I trust nor doubt if I know everything. There are, after all, reasons to doubt; and to discard prior beliefs on the basis of new discovery itself is a species of learning, so that knowledge of my past errors is just as much an antiskeptical realization as it is cautionary. One can develop a certain critical skepticism as a guard against naive trust, but one must equally respect the critical powers in terms of their enlightenment. We are thus not only trusting and doubting beings, we are also learners from our own errors. Learning therefore becomes the link between doubting and trusting on the one hand and knowing and ignorance on the other. To ask what do I doubt thus confronts us with this realization: no account of certainty as an attitude nor the certitude of apodictic claims is ever sufficient in itself to bridge the existential gap between knowing and ignorance on the one and doubting and trusting on the other. Even though we must be fairly harsh with Descartes, we learn from his asking that to be able to doubt frees us from noncritical acceptance or naivete. To ask what enables this doubting is thus fundamental.

The professor asks a student to imagine two isosceles right triangles. The student agrees to do this. The professor then asks him to arrange these two triangles against each other so that they share a common hypotenuse. The student performs this maneuver in his imagination. "What image must you see?" the professor then asks. "I see, and indeed I must see, a square." That we can do such a thing is entirely remarkable and unexpected. Consider it simply as a phenomenon that can and does occur. At no time is any reference made to an inference or a rule. Except for the noncontroversial assumption that the student knows what the terms mean, there is no use of concepts or principles. Yet, the student rightly recognizes that he not only has produced a square, but that, following the request merely to imagine things, and to look in his mind at what he imagines, he must see a square. The conjunction of *must* with *see* already seems unusual, since what I see apparently presents me merely with what is the case, not with what must be the case. We must sequester, for the moment, the protest that modern mathematics can be taught as algorithmic, that there are other ways of showing geometric truths than imagining figures in my head. One can indeed carry out a discipline using rules and concepts that would produce similar realizations; as, for example, the claim that geometry is analytic, and that squares can be defined in terms of two adjacent right triangles. These alternative possibilities, however, are irrelevant, for the fact remains that we can imagine two right isosceles triangles sharing a common hypotenuse and from this act of imagination realize that the conjoined figure is a square. Merely because other people do other things does not mean I cannot do this one.

If, however, I can indeed perform, in my imagination, this and similar maneuvers, I must as a philosopher ask how it is possible. In a sense, though, we already know how it is possible. We are able to imagine things in our mind that we do indeed, in some sense, look at. To look at, is, in the unhappy translation of Kant's *anschauen*, to intuit. I intuit directly my own spatial images. I do not analyze the properties of right triangles and squares and, on the basis of these analyses, conclude that the conjoined triangles logically must form a square. If we say that the newly constructed image does not follow from a mere study of definitions, then this conjunction reveals something beyond those definitional concepts. Accordingly, Kant calls the resulting judgment synthetic. Since I do this without relying on an external drawing, it is purely within my own mental powers, specifically the imagination, and, since the result is not merely optional, but necessary, Kant calls it a priori. The point is: we do these things; they are actions we perform. Kant asks: How are these synthetic a priori judgments, conceived not as propositions, but as acts, possible? And in asking this, Kant violently altered forever the history of thought.

The German word *vermögen* in its verbal sense means: to be able to (do); in its substantive sense, it thus means the power or enabling to do something. English translators use the term *faculty* to refer to this enablement, thereby losing some of the original flavor of what Kant means. How, he asks, am I enabled to conjoin two triangles so that I must see them as constituting—making up—a square?

That we can do geometry has long been one of the most remarkable, even surprising, facts about the human species. Arithmetic may be more useful; certainly it is more basic since it is assumed even by geometers; yet it is geometry and not arithmetic that seems to have fascinated all thinkers from the very beginning. Even those worshipers of arithmetic numbers, the Pythagoreans, sought to understand numeric cosmology in geometric terms. The Renaissance saw in geometry not its epistemic power or even its utility but its beauty. Every major advance in the history of physics was preceded by earlier advances in geometry. It pleases the eye even as it satisfies the mind; high school sophomores draw circles with compasses and measure angles with protractors and change themselves entirely by the realization of that power within themselves to be so authoritative. What, then, does it mean to ask for its enablement? Who are we that we can do such things?

Kant's answer, of course, is to ask what it means to be conscious; and he finds we are conscious in three differing but interconnected ways: to be able to receive, i.e., receptivity, which is called the sensibility (and includes imagining); to connect, which is called the understanding; and to make and give rules, called reason. His answers, however brilliant, are not as astonishing as his asking, for he asks about enablement *directly*. He does not ask whether we do geometry or science or morality, he asks what enables us to do them. He does not ask what the world is like, nor what can be doubted, nor about the origins of ideas; he more deeply asks: How am I enabled to do such things? He seeks, in other words, for their possibility lurking within their actuality.

Geometry, as opposed to arithmetic, can be seen. Indeed, geometry in its original sense, cannot only be seen, but constructed. That we are able to calculate abstractly from these origins does not change the significance of this seeing. We see the two right triangles, brought together, making a square. This is unlike most seeing; indeed, it is so unlike most seeing many thinkers have assumed it cannot be the product of seeing. How can we see, in the literal, visual sense of seeing, that something must be seen in a specific way? However we answer this, we already realize, perhaps uncomfortably, that we cannot think about our seeing in traditional ways any longer; for now, seeing itself seems to provide us with necessary realizations. Yet, it is not only the remarkable discovery that seeing is now authoritative that Kant's asking has produced. Consider his analysis of the judgments themselves as a priori and synthetic. What does it mean to ask about the ways we make judgments? This is reflection of the highest order, for it is a reflection on our own linguistic acts as phenomena, and not abstractly considered propositions. Kant did not originate the distinction between a priori and a posteriori; nor was he the first to discern the difference between analysis and synthesis—breaking things apart in order to understand, and bringing things together in order to understand. Kant was the first, however, to see the need to fuse these two pairs of distinctions together; and he realized, with this discovery, that a new way of asking was now made possible. He began to make clear just why it is that geometry has always been so wondrous: our seeing reveals itself.

It is difficult to decide which is the more remarkable: Kant's method of asking or his creative discernment of what our seeing entails. They are, of course, interconnected. It is only by asking critically in terms of our enablement that the true nature of geometry is revealed. What Kant discovered was that the magnificent spectacle of geometry as a source of awe and wonder, from its earliest Egyptian beginnings to its lofty regime under Euclid, and on to its rediscovery as pivotal to the Renaissance, in fact is based in the nature of geometry itself. For bringing authority to vision is also what we mean by the beautiful, particularly beauty in the visual arts. Geometry, as seen, is aesthetic in the sense that no calculus or logic can be—not even as arithmetic can be. Indeed, Kant's analysis of the beautiful uses the same language: that which is seen in such a way that authority, in the form of universality, is discerned in our very seeing.

There is something awesome about Kant's analysis that is independent of its accuracy. We often use the metaphor of "digging deeply" to refer to philosophical penetration that provides us with unexpected illumination; and to some extent what is remarkable here is the depth of Kant's digging. What cannot be overlooked, however, is that this depth is achieved by a new and fundamental asking that leaves us almost breathless in its power to reveal. It is an asking that is a species of metaphoric digging. To ask fundamentally is thus, by suggestion, to dig deeply—to get at the roots or even the taproot. It is only the insignificant who are unmoved by the sheer revelatory power of Kant's asking. What he has shown is that the deepest digging uncovers the taproot: the enabling of the already actual. Whatever makes possible what is already wondrous in actuality is even more wondrous.

There is, in Heidegger's remarkable question, an almost childlike freshness. We can ask why there are trees and why there are potholes, so why not ask why there is anything at all? To ask this way may well be a species of hubris, for it seems to demand that reasons can be given on the highest level of all—and if reason cannot contribute to this asking, why is it worth having? Heidegger quickly assures us that this use of the term *why* is neither asking for motives, purposes, or even explanations in the sense of supportive accounts. Rather, he claims, the *why* becomes a question of meaning—and specifically it becomes an asking about what it means to be at all. It is our privilege, granted by this inquiry, to ask what it means—or how it is possible—to ask in this way. We do exist; surely nothing should prohibit us from asking what it means to exist. Just as I can do geometry and ask what it means to do it, or fall in love and ask what it means to do so, or commit a wrong and ask what it means—so my own being itself can be questioned in terms of its meaning.

It is at this phase that the childlike wonder is transmogrified into a most adult seriousness and awe. The term *meaning* seems to have taken on the quality of a chanted mantra or mystic shibboleth. What can *meaning* possibly mean if it is to be taken in all philosophical seriousness? When critically examined it turns out that Heidegger's asking is as far from mysticism as one can possibly get. What is meant by *meaning* is thinkability: the meaning of such seductive phenomena as suffering, loving, being guilty, or even speaking itself, is what enables us to think—not opine or feel—about them. And we do think about these phenomena. The problem is, we also feel and opine and guess and have superstitious attitudes toward them; and part of the task of thinking is to distinguish thinking about these phenomena from merely opining or guessing about them. This is not unusual: we feel, opine, guess, and have superstitions about science, the law, logic, marriage, and philosophy itself—and everyone realizes there is a difference between thinking about such institutions and having feelings about them, and part of our job as thinkers is to straighten out these differences, or perhaps in some cases, to synthesize them. To ask if we truly can think about such phenomena is answered by the fact that we do think about them; and the same answer must be given to the existential skeptic who uses scorn or contempt as a dismissive tool. We do think about being. Indeed we can and do ask what it means to be at all. And since we do, we come face to face with the question of the meaning of being, wondering critically what being means and hence why there is anything whatsoever, understanding by this a raising of those same modalities that haunt all fundamental asking: If we are contingent, yet capable of thinking about necessity, how are we to think about our own being in light of our own being able to be?

To appreciate this, a comparison with the prior asking may be helpful. Kant, we learn, asks a new and profound question: How is something possible? Heidegger realizes the depth of his asking, perhaps more than any other critic of Kant ever has; but he wonders whether even this way of asking is fundamental. Consider the two ways of asking: How is geometry possible? What does it mean to do geometry? The latter asking is enabled by the first, and the first still has its stamp upon the second. To ask what it means to do geometry must include asking how it is possible; but it considers this enablement more deeply. And, by asking more deeply about enablement, we find this asking perforce coming to grips with issues that had been lurking in the shadows. What enables geometry is our power to imagine space as an object of consciousness—no mean feat in itself. But now we must ask: What, though, does it mean to imagine? What does it mean to be spatial? And we must note the power of this shift. We no longer ask only how to look at space, but what it means to be in space. We certainly can and do think about what it means to be in space; but it does not take long to realize that however this is thought about, it reveals—whether we like it or not—part of what it means to be at all. This shift or deepening of our understanding of what enables geometry reflects Heidegger's entire existential-ontological approach. It is necessary, however, to see more precisely how this move generates out of the original question.

If there is something both exciting and beckoning about asking why there is anything rather than nothing, it is in part due to the very first word. And so we ask: Why *why?* To ask why is to ask on the most intimate level of our own ability to ask at all, and hence to initiate originally the act of reasoning. At the earliest stages of our self-realization, the one thing we know directly is our own motivation, though not always the specific motive or motives. We know why we hit our sibling—she hit me first! We know why we pull up the covers—to make us warm. We know why we run to our mother—because we are afraid. Since we know, however vaguely, our own motivation, we express most of our wondering in these terms, much to the chagrin of parents. Why does it thunder? Why do we sleep? Why am I afraid? It does not take us long to realize that many answers to our asking why are given, not in the sense of motivation, but of explanation. Why put a lid on the pan? To keep the soup warm. There is, of course, still an underlying motive—we want the soup warm—but the action is explained in terms of design, in the sense of a project. Efficient causal explanation stems from this originary sense of asking, and is ultimately subservient to it just because efficient causality asks solely in terms of events that happen, not in terms of minds that project plans or seek satisfaction in projective explanations and motives. It is for this reason that Aristotle ranks purpose as the ultimate explanation (*aitia*).

It was Kant, of course, who recognized most clearly that we can think purposively without thinking a specific purpose—which explains both aesthetic judgments and allows for ultimate asking *about* nature without demanding specific purposes or designs *in* nature. The childlike wonder that greets us when we ask why anything rather than nothing may well rely on our expectation that the most intimate and immediate sense of reasoning is personal motivation, and as long as this can be seen as figurative or analogic, there is no harm in it. The why question remains fundamental even when we realize that it contains within it the very possibility of what it means to ask at all. What begins most intimately with asking *why* in terms of our personal motives, develops into the realization that *why* also asks for explanations; and the ensuing delight we take merely in explanations as explanations, and not merely as useful accounts, allows us to realize that purposiveness, which entails meaning, need not always have a specific purpose. Why is there anything? then, becomes What does it mean for anything to be at all? Since *meaning* here signifies that which enables thought, the question is now stunning: How can we think at all about being and not being? This formulation, however, since it is ultimate, cannot be resolved merely by reference to a faculty. It must rather be confronted in terms of our *own* being as it is manifested to us in original asking. Thus the original intimacy is retained, but no longer in terms of interests, but in terms of thinkability or meaning.

Still, there is a sense of the original formulation that persists. To ask why there is anything makes us wonder in the original, intimate way, as if we were asking: Who would want there to be anything rather than nothing? Is there something worthwhile about being? Is there, somehow, a real possibility here, as if a choice were made: there could have been nothing, so why is there something? Does it make as much sense for there to be nothing as it does for there to be something? Perhaps on the purely logical level, for there to be nothing is no more or no less compelling than for there to be something; but this would suggest the entire, blooming universe is the result of sheer serendipity, not only original but ongoing.

The antiexistential critic here is most ingenious: such questions, they say, being unanswerable, are improper questions. We may think we are asking coherently, but when analyzed carefully the questions reveal themselves as subtle forms of anthropomorphism, akin to asking if the rock really wants to be lying on the hillside. Perhaps, but this indictment may be challenged by a counter-indictment of nihilism. Are we reduced to this childishness— two sides calling each other nasty names, like politicians at election time? To ask if it makes as much sense for there to be something or nothing may be neither anthropomorphic nor unanswerable, especially if it leads us to consider what it means to be—the ultimate metaphysical question. To consider whether there is a reason for anything existing rather than nothing is to raise an entirely legitimate question about the limits of our reasoning. It is, after all, a question. What is illegitimate is to force the questioner to entertain only two dread possibilities: nihilism or anthropomorphism. To give any reasons at all may strike some critics as already being anthropomorphic, which is ridiculous; to realize there may be some mysteries inherent in our universe may strike other critics as being nihilistic—which is also ridiculous. The critic must do his job but one need not be disarmed by the probings.

It may yet seem suspiciously anthropomorphic, however, to allow the original question to drift, as an unanchored boat, into the uncharted waters of asking whether it is better to be than not, or whether there is an inherent choice in being over not being. Terms such as *better* and *choice* seem unsanctioned in such deep seas. Yet, to dismiss such considerations simply because they risk losing the credentials of putative disinterest, may elicit an even greater risk: that of asking disingenuously. We do, after all, consider our own existing at times as a choice—as when we consider suicide or engage in great risks. We also consider whether certain things are worth existing, as when we wonder about the loss of a species, the destruction of a fetus, or whether the courage to go on living in dreadful circumstances is a genuine virtue or a mere prejudice. These are meaningful considerations; but we do indeed raise them in terms of what it means to be. One of the powerful contributions of Heidegger is his re-fusing the questions of worth with the question of being. It is not necessary to decide in advance whether there is worth in being; but it is paramount to ask whether there may be. In this way, Heidegger's existential discovery of Kant's asking about enablement thrills in part just because it opens up new ways of synthesis. By his analyses, we are forced to reconsider the traditional disjunctions between worth and being, and the authority of his asking prohibits us from simply dismissing these possibilities on the basis of an Enlightenment prejudice.

The two most powerful animal sentiments necessary for survival are fear and lust; the former enables the survival of the individual, the latter, the species. Were it not for fear we would fall prey to every peril; were fear not to compel us to run from the tiger, we would be eaten. It is folly, then, not to fear. Were it not for lust, there would be no following generation; the future would be merely our death. Yet, for that species capable of civility, we have developed resistances to these feral, needful urgencies that are deeply troubling. They are also curiously glorious—there is no other word; they glorify. Courage is nothing else but a glorious way of being afraid; concealment ironically glorifies the beauty in our nakedness. It seems singularly fitting that these two final questions that enable fundamental asking should come from literature; one dramatic, the other sacred. Asking happens beyond the dubious boundaries of any discipline. These specific questions are chosen because of the wealth they provide for those who share in their digging.

Hamlet fears his own fearing. Or, to be more precise, he fears he may fear badly. As are we, the audience, Hamlet is rightly puzzled about what dread narcotic has numbed his resolve; but though it fascinates us to speculate on why the prince cannot act, overemphasis on the cause distracts from the drama. Hamlet may wonder why he is impotent, but the nature of the cause is of intense dramatic relevance only if it can be ascribed to his own cowardice. This he fears more profoundly than his failure to avenge his father. It is bad enough not to avenge, but if the reason is a disguised cravenness, he must loathe himself more than he loathes Claudius. It is precisely because we the audience are convinced by Shakespeare's dramaturgic skill that Hamlet is truly noble and hence not a poltroon, that we wonder so delightfully why he yet does not act; but it is the young prince's agony over his own doubts as to his true courage that grips us in a radiant rapture that only the greatest of artworks can provide. In doubting his own courage we find a splendid resource for understanding what courage means, and why courage is itself so fundamental in understanding who we are. Even when Hamlet adumbrates Nietzsche in a cry that villainizes the very mentor of our souls by suggesting that "conscience doth make cowards of us all," we see the revelatory depth of his torment. It may even be true.

It is not the peculiarity of his unique and unhappy position that thwarts; it is the very nature of courage itself. No mere definitionalist approach, as is found in the early part of Plato's *Laches*, can tell us why nobly fearing—courage—is so fundamental. Nevertheless a few reminders as to the nature of this paradoxical virtue may be permitted. The claim can be made that courage is the original virtue, for what would it mean to care about justice were we to lack the sand to confront the unjust, to right the wrong, fight against the tyrant, or to abet all other wrongs by the milky vice of the craven? What good is wisdom if I am too weak to face it; what is piety if I dare not defend what is mine? Indeed, it takes courage to confront courage. In some ways, being courageous is being oneself; for if who I am matters, that I matter prompts my willingness to risk; if I do not matter, then neither does my being a coward—an insouciance that guarantees retreat.

There is an ironic paradox in all courage; for if I am not frightened, if I do not tremble in dread before the terrible, there is no courage at all. The more frightened I am, the greater the courage. To be able to be craven thus seems an ironic necessity if the virtue is to be possible. At the same time the irony reshapes itself with the realization that what is most greatly feared is being craven; thus it is fear that leads us to ignominious defeat and fear of ignominy that is the truth of courage. What, then, is the nature of this ennobling fear that fears fearing? Both the courageous and the coward fear; this is but common wisdom. What transcends the common is the discovery that courage is not the overcoming of fear but, paradoxically and ironically, the deepening of it. In ordinary fear what I dread is injury, pain, or death; in great fear what I dread is diminishment. Perhaps we are simply too proud to allow ourselves to be disquantitied, shrunk to mere shadows of our reality, mocked into a shameful meekness by our own censure. It is this self-mockery and shame that the noble fears most, precisely because, in originating it in ourselves, it disables rather than enables; and in disabling, it makes us less.

Being able to fear is thus the origin of both the virtue and the vice; the difference is in the nature of the enablement. Being able to fear well rests upon fearing what I am able to become; fearing badly rests upon what might be done to me. The latter is not merely external and the former internal: that is, the coward does not merely fear external threats and the courageous merely fear internal threats—though there is some truth in saying this. Rather, it is further revealed that the very nature of the threat matters: Is the threat of abusing or being abused? Do I abuse myself, in fearing badly, or am I abused but intact, fearing well? The virtue of courage thus reveals our own existence in terms of its enablement.

The critic may hesitate at this, and protest that the argument, even if valid, has brought us inevitably to the more ultimate presupposition: Is it possible for us to be the origin of fearing well and fearing badly unless we are free agents? Are we not now confronted with the agonizing analysis of the free will? For surely, unless I am free, I cannot be said to be able to fear one way or the other. This protest is of supreme importance, for the present emphasis on fundamental asking here confronts a formidable adversary. *It is not freedom that makes courage possible, but courage that makes freedom possible.* It is far, far nobler to reflect on the concrete, available phenomenon of our own fearing than on the abstract possibilities of two contending metaphysical speculations, determinism and voluntarism. The construction of these opposing *isms*, and their consequent attacks on their opponents is not fundamental—indeed, cannot be fundamental, since, being speculative, it rests upon abstract possibilities rather than concrete possibilities within the actual, existential confrontation of our own real fear. Whether there is a metaphysical entity called a will becomes, at best, a mere clumsy attempt to ground explanations in some entity, that maddeningly must remain beyond any concrete availability, and hence beyond any worthy basis for deciding. What matters here is the asking; and if the asking is fundamental it far outranks any metaphysical speculations. For the point is this: it is not some metaphysical entity that accounts for such depth of thinking, it is Hamlet—and hence ourselves—asking whether we be called a coward, and if so, then also a villain and a scullion. Hamlet asks on the level of fundamental reality; the theoretical voluntarist or determinist provides formal possibilities that, of themselves, are unanchored to truth. Courage, when deeply asked, cannot be diminished by the cowardice of lesser asking.

Definitionalist refining and speculating on philosophical presuppositions are worthy endeavors, but they are not fundamental; and unless they are grounded on the enablement of fundamental asking, they are empty. Suppose we ask what it means to be free. If we suggest that being free means having options from which we choose our preference, we either reduce freedom to the mere satisfaction of whims or we assume a faculty that relies for its assumption on contrary-to-fact conditionals, which are always insecure as evidence. Suppose we claim every event must have a cause and only events are real. This begs the question, for such a claim already denies the possibility of a meaningful freedom; and indeed the claim itself is easily denied. If, however, by freedom we mean being able to resist inclinations to which we ought not yield, freedom now becomes meaningful rather than metaphysically speculative. But even this improvement is not adequate, for no matter how precise our analysis, what seems always lacking in any account is why one wills badly or wills well. If one suggests, as Kant does, that being good is willing as we ought—the only absolutely good thing is a good will— then we leave unanswered why one person wills well and another wills badly. So why even talk about wills at all?

Courage, however, is real. We know what it means to fear in a way that enslaves us, and we know what it means to fear nobly—when what we fear is slavery itself. Hamlet asks if, being a coward, he is a villain or a scullion. Both terms denote baseness. *Scullion* comes from the word for broom; *villain* comes from *village*. A mere broom-sweeper, or a low villager, is, in the social strata of the day, not free—they were mere serfs or slaves. Certainly they were not free in the technical sense of freeman—nobles. Thus, the princely Hamlet fears being a scullion or a villain precisely because adopting such baseness would deprive him of freedom and dignity. The direct confrontation of this enablement is courage. Being free is not the abstract possibility of having options but confronting fear with a higher fear. We can reflect upon a troubled youth required to do a fearsome duty, such as venturing down an ill-lit, gang-infested street to help a friend. He fears two things: being set upon by ruthless gangs who may beat him or even kill him; and he fears yielding to the first fear in a cowardly way. The nobler fear is the second, and courage is the name we give to that fearing. The philosophical priority is thus revealed.

Yet, even now the asking must be pressed. It is not the question of how we define courage, nor even to question what it means to confront fear, although this latter is a better formulation. No, the question that enables fundamental asking is still Hamlet's and hence ours: Am I a coward? To ask this is to confront our own enablement. Even in asking it we already manifest the possibility, for it takes courage even to ask it; it takes courage even to pray for courage; and in asking and praying for courage we become in part courageous. Indeed, even when we fail, and wearily take up the venture once again, bruised with the dread realization that we once acted in a cowardly way, but perhaps able yet to find a strength within ourselves, this also is being courageous. Only from this originary phenomenon of direct enablement that we call courage is any meaningful sense of freedom possible. Denying this enablement is cowardice. It is a modality fit only for scullery sweepers and low, undignified villagers—that is, slaves—never forgetting that such scullions may wear a regal crown, or that humble workers may do noble acts.

Asking if we be cowards thus makes us able to be free. If such asking is rare, or unavailable in philosophy texts, the shame is on us for lacking the boldness to ask fundamentally.

The last of these questions may be the most denuding—and the pun is deliberate. Are we not naked unless we are told? Is there anything more mysterious than this curious ambivalence we have toward revealing and concealing ourselves? Even among the most staid puritans are many who recognize the legitimacy of nudes in art; even among the most licentious are those who take offense at the illegitimate voyeur. On the frieze of the Greek temple the naked warriors are the barbarians; on the floor of the same temple the naked athletes are deemed beauteous. We know there are nudists that dwell in camps who reject the fig leaf that others say is the essence of civilization; we know of the overdressed who "go native" when confronted by seemingly easygoing tribes. Most of us sense there is a genuine difference between pornography and artistry, though we hesitate to articulate by statute what the difference is. Many feel a delightful freedom in shedding their clothes, yet would never offend by doing so in public places. Yet, why be naked unless we can be looked at? Why does the artist almost instinctively sketch out the human figure undraped? If some young bodies are beautiful—and surely they are—why should there ever be shame or modesty?

Is it possible that the traditional accounts are simply backward? Perhaps modesty itself is the greatest realization of the body's beauty, that the pornographer makes the same body ugly and hence unattractive, that art does not present us without lust but with intensified carnality, that only with the possibility of shame can we be freely naked, that beauty is not safely enframed by distance, but direct in nearness? Even were we to entertain this suggestion, however, it does us little good, for the bold, unavoidable conflict remains. Why do we hide ourselves? Why do we reveal ourselves? What does it mean that we ourselves can look at, and be looked at, so as to induce shame?

The temptations here for the inquirer are vast. We want to discuss beauty and its relation to truth. We know there is much to be found in the analysis of culture, of art, of sexuality and intimacy, of great personal pleasure and the possible distinction between pleasure and gratification. We want to know if there are moral dimensions to being naked. We want to know of the radical distinction between moral guilt and existential shame. Yet, tempting as all these worthy topics may be, they must be resisted. The original question loses its originality when distracted from its palpable and immediate power. In the myth of the Garden, Adam and Eve were unclothed from the beginning; nor were they so dense as to be unaware of it. They were, for all that, not yet naked, however. Being naked is entirely antipodal to being simply, naturally, unclad. In Milton's epic, the poet says of Adam: "he covered, but his robe/Uncovered more." With this poetic insight, we are required to take a fresh look, for there is too much that matters here.

We conceal. We reveal. We conceal in our revealing and reveal in our concealing. Yet, these are not merely acts that we perform: hiding and uncovering are modalities of our very existence. We hide, in part, to protect that precious, irreducible privacy that is ours alone. That this hiding reveals our need to hide is inescapable, and deeply ironic; for in hiding we reveal what most we want hidden. Yet, even this is ironic, for in erotic disclosure we also want this privacy to be shared. Yet being naked makes us common with the species; we really are all alike underneath. This is the existential realization of the ancient problem of the one and the many: we do not first wonder how the single term *hill* can be applied to all the mounds we climb; but we do sense very deeply the truth that we can somehow lose ourselves into an unwholesome whole, that we matter beyond our species, that no label or reductionist simple can grasp our essence, that we are radically unique yet belong to the world. The single term *naked* implies vulnerability as well as desirability, private yet public, innocence and rapine, vulgar, yet noble.

It is a monumental discovery that this hiding and revealing, this vulnerability of uniqueness, preciousness in the midst of commonality, is truth itself. When Lear looks at the "naked fellow," Mad Tom—Edgar disguised by his nakedness—he says, "Thou art the thing itself." The troubled King then seeks to tear off his own garments in a desperate attempt to get at the truth—the answer to his own question, "Who is Lear?" Truth, as Heidegger reveals, is uncovering, but in a wrenching irony that palls all normal understanding of irony; for never are we laid more bare than in our covering, and in this need to cover we are denuded, and truth as such happens for the first time. The language here is not the moral language of deceiving others, or even the deeper wrong of self-deceit. It is rather the existential language of knowingly hiding ourselves—and this, in the most vivid sense of hiding our bodies, as if the body's nakedness discloses or enables the soul.

The suggestion is thus made: perhaps this curious phenomenon of unnatural shame, this alluring bewilderment at the ambivalence of being naked is nothing other than our enabling of truth. I do not mean to suggest a mere symbol or symptom, nor a mere cultural icon, nor even a moral sentiment. The suggestion, if it is to mean anything, must be bolder: the covering and revealing of ourselves simply is the original phenomenon of truth mattering. To suggest this requires reflection on the passage, "Who told thee thou wert naked?" What does telling have to do with it? Why are we able to be naked only when told we are? Does not this very dependence on being told suggest that it is artificial? Or is it the other way around: that only what is told, only what is articulated in language, can be true; and so our nakedness, the first thing we must be told in order for it to be true, is the first thing that *can* be true? Perhaps it is language that strips us bare. Perhaps even bolder: only if we can cover ourselves in shame can we speak at all, since pseudo-language is merely communication—and hence not really language—until our being revealed, stripped naked, matters. Only if truth matters can we matter, but we can hide ourselves only if we matter. We must be told we are naked because nothing in our innocence could possibly reveal our truth.

The question is somewhat rhetorical, of course, since the answer is so enigmatic. We are the ones who tell ourselves we are naked. Even in the Garden myth it is not the serpent who tells Adam and Eve they are naked; they tell themselves. This is important just because there are camp-nudists and neosavages and indifferentists who shrug the whole story off as a remnant of puritanical times. There are those who feel shame is the only shameful thing. Those who are indifferently unclothed have not told themselves they are naked and hence are without shame, and hence are without the enabling of truth. Truth, then, is not natural, nor innocent. It is rather a loss of innocence, enabling through its loss the authenticity of guilt and the first chapter of the strange saga of our learning to look at ourselves.

Who tells us we are naked? Once we realize that only we ourselves can tell us, the truest shame begins. But once we realize we are the ones whose looking and then telling strips us, we also enable the glorious possibility; we turn away from the naked barbarians on the frieze and look at the naked athletes on the temple floor. The shame enables the glory. There is absolutely no innocence in seeing these splendid figures. Innocence, as its etymology suggests, is a species of blindness, of not merely not knowing but being unable to know, unable to see—and most specifically, unable to see ourselves. To ask who calls us naked thus enables the very possibility of truth. What can be more fundamental than this?

11

Mystery

It is not strange that, being finite, we should find the world somewhat mysterious. What is the strangest of our strange ways is that we are most mysterious to ourselves. The Delphic injunction to know thyself suggests that self-knowledge is curiously elusive; and our lack of this virtue is due not to ordinary ignorance about facts concerning who we are, but rests on our artful skill in keeping our secrets hidden even from our own probing. Hamlet offers Guildenstern a recorder, and asks him to play upon the instrument. The hapless Guildenstern protests he lacks the skill; he "knows not the stops." Hamlet then upbraids him for trying to play on him as if he were a pipe, and scolds him for trying "to pluck out the heart of his mystery." Fundamental asking, however, does not seek to pluck out the heart of our mystery; if anything it seeks to retain the mystery as a resource for truth. We ask, not to excise our mystery, but to understand what it means. It is precisely because tearing out the heart of our mystery violates who we are and hence is an enemy to truth and not a friend, that fundamental asking reveals more than any answer, though we must be reminded that all true asking is already an indirect answering, that it reveals truth, and that we are wiser in the asking than we were before we asked. To title this inquiry the asking mystery is thus to suggest two meanings: first, that in asking fundamentally we realize that the fundamental is itself somewhat mysterious, else why ask about it; second, that our asking itself is somewhat mysterious, as if we are never quite sure what enables us to ask in the first place. The term *mystery* here is not meant in the sense of a mere puzzle or problem as yet unsolved; nor does it mean incoherence or irrationality; neither does it mean something which must be accepted or rejected solely on a whim or act of faith, nor does it suggest something exclusively available only to the anointed few. Rather, mystery in its philosophical sense means that lure within truth itself that lures us to the truth even as it deepens its need to ask.

The lure of asking is truth. We ourselves, in asking, become an essential part of that truth. These suggestions are doubtless paradoxes in some sense, perhaps they are even ironic; but they do not offend most thinkers precisely because most of us recognize they may be true in themselves. What is not obvious is *whom* we ask. It may seem obvious that who we ask about asking is ourselves, but here the obvious obfuscates. Or rather, it is obviously true that we do ask ourselves about asking, but this obviousness somehow deceives. David's magnificent question, we say glibly enough, presupposes God's existence, which enables him to ask God what man is such that God would care about him. What is now suggested, however, is that David's question is more fundamental than whether God exists. I cannot ask whether God exists without first having some idea of what is meant by God and what it means for there to be God. David's question is more fundamental because it asks about why we think God in the first place. The poet confesses astonishment that he, unworthy of necessity and lacking finality, should nonetheless be, as asker, ranked between what is beyond and what is beneath, yet remaining curiously intimate with both of these. God then, is the asked, the mysteriously asked; and as such God enables David's asking.

Does this reflection indicate that since it is obvious that we ask ourselves about asking, and God is the asked, that we have created God as some extension of ourselves, in order to anchor fundamental asking in some externalist metaphysical harbor? Even to suggest such an anthropomorphism already retreats from the truth revealed in David's fundamental asking: we have, by asking such a comfortable if dreary question lost sight of the original, uncomfortable urgency. We cannot ask David's question as our own if we insist first on asking this shadowy question made entirely of abstract deceits. If we insist on answering before asking, we claim that David's prior "belief" in God accounts for his interesting question being raised in the theological manner that we falsely assume lies in the psalms. This is about David the insignificant rather than David the magnificent. Are we then compelled to "believe" in David's God if we maintain that his asking is truly fundamental? This is about us the insignificant rather than us touched by the magnificent. It is akin to sitting next to a new acquaintance during a glorious performance of the Immolation Scene of Wagner's *Götterdämmerung*, and hearing him ask, How much does all this cost?

He will not be our acquaintance for long. The production does cost something, and the question of its expense needs sometime to be asked. But such asking is not what it means to hear and witness such greatness, and it is the greatness that makes it worth the cost. There is mystery in David's question; and there is even mystery in Wagner's music, for it is explicable only in terms of genius. David's asking is more fundamental than asking whether God exists just because his asking shows what it means for there to be a meaningful hearer who can be asked about why we matter. There is no record in the psalm of any divine response; it remains a mystery—that is, it lures us to truth enabled only by asking reverently in the presence of the awesome.

To ask about asking is mysterious in part since it confronts our own inability to see ourselves except in reflectors, but the mystery does not prohibit inquiry altogether. The problem is how to raise the question. Do we ask it in Kantian terms: By what faculty do we ask fundamentally? To paraphrase Nietzsche's unfair remark, the only meaningful answer to this would be the asking faculty, whatever that is. What good does that do us? Do we ask it in terms of its epistemic success? Such success can and must be given only in answers, thwarting the enterprise from the start. Do we consider psychological motives? They are vague, multifarious, and unreliable. Do we ask it in terms of an overall metaphysical system? Whether the system is truly "overall" is part of the question itself. Perhaps then, we might ask it in existential terms: What does it mean to ask? This suggestion has some merit, but it, too, is problematic. How do we make the first step? The language of this inquiry suggests one possible approach—we might ask: What enables fundamental asking? Enablement itself seems grounded in our being possible as actual, but the danger here is that the initiation of the inquiry itself still seems as dark as ever. Perhaps we are asking too directly. In light of the Genesis question about nakedness in the previous chapter, it may be needful to uncover by covering, and ask, at least provisionally, the opposite question: What disables us from asking fundamentally? In indirection, then, a boldness is perhaps fitting. I suggest the enemies to such asking are the busy and the free. The former may not seem so remarkable, but the latter seems irreverent. Can the free be an enemy to asking? Or if it is so, then perhaps asking is thereby indicted. If the free is the ultimate basis of worth, and fundamental asking is inimical to it, then perhaps we should not ask at all.

But first to business. How many poets, essayists, philosophers, and even social critics have warned us of this? We are distracted by noise. The concerns for acquiring wealth, extending survival, wallpapering over the slatted walls of social acceptance, muting or relieving our urgencies—all rattle violently in the tin pail of the everyday, creating a din of such eclipsing volume that all hearing is abused, demoted to visceral reaction, as with the young dancing to heavy rhythms, identifying themselves solely with savage pulsations. Whatever is whispered is unnoticed, and truth-revealing language is usurped by the shrieking of television newscasts and the obscenity of commercial advertising. We speak to sell, we listen to buy: such is the essence of speech. We know this only too well, yet knowing it does not enable escape. A species of this loud commercialism is sadly found in the overeager reach for answers in the marketplace of academic labels. Truth itself becomes a business with many tiers of caste and snobbery. Opinions are hawked from cheap, sidewalk vendors; but theories are sold more dearly in malls, where the goods are wrapped in packages bearing international logos. Weltanschauungen are sold only in the finest shop, boxed in discrete silver-coated cartons with a bow. Philosophies are the highest commerce, sold in stocks and shares on the floor of the exchanges, where all is paper or electronic pulses, marked by the rise and fall of the Dow-Jones, producing, aside from unearned wealth and even more noise, nothing at all. This image itself is cheaply made. There are many who toil honestly and care for truth, but the clamor of business unfortunately spills its toxicity even among the sweet waters of the sincere. If none are entirely immune however, then neither are all entirely unarmed. To know the enemy is vital for good strategy as well as tactics. The noise would sell us answers, the busy forfeits all quiet, but if the secrets of truth are found only in whispered asking, we must outmaneuver the enemy if we cannot defeat them. We need not buy.

Yet, *busy* has another meaning, though akin. Being busy means doing something—not being idle. This peril we also know well; the tocsin against it is an entreaty to silence, the uncommercial, and to reflection. We call the peril distraction, suggesting that we have taken the wrong path, or that we have forgotten why we are here in the first place. If the busy distracts from asking it is because of its success. The busy get things done. Leisure becomes recreation—that is, it makes us better workers. Answers, after all, give us something to work with—distracting us by this subtle use of the word *work*. "I'm working hard" the thinker says and does not realize he lies. Philosophical asking is a species of what the Greeks called *schole*—leisure. That we get paid while we ask—and never because we ask—may be right enough; that we do it to get paid is not right at all. The Socratic warning against the Sophists is still relevant and deserves reiteration even if it be commonly known. No lasting harm will result from this paragraph.

It is the second suggestion, now that we have "done with business"—as the busy would say, ironically—that is more disturbing. How is the free the enemy of asking? Precisely because asking enslaves us, however briefly. Or as one rapt in the thrall of passion, feeling owned by the beloved, embracing the ligatures that bind and the chains that fetter, might say—oh, let this slavery last. There is so much irony here that it inebriates. Being free is itself a species of bondage, for its essence is responsibility, and being responsible incarcerates us in the moral prison of our actions. To promise binds me to a future that may imperil or harm, yet it is only as free that the promise is possible. The free act of promising unfrees that act of tomorrow. It is easier to sense the irony than to understand it, but the rapture of its bondage may help us soar. What, we ask, now chastened by these unchaste reflections, does it mean to be free? If we listen carefully to the preachers of liberty, what do we hear?

Cut loose these shackles that bind you to your home. Let no man nor woman, no hearth nor native land, no belief that fosters, no system that organizes, nor threat that unifies, no uninvited duty nor unquestioned trust ensnare you. Be rather yourself the sole guardian of your interests, your concerns, your beliefs, your loves, your loyalty, your devotion. Sever all cords that tie you to anyone, shun the prisoner's garb of belonging, the uniforms that unify, the clothes that others weave, spotting you as this or that. It is better to be lonely and free than sharing and unfree. Select only those comrades who let you be yourself, and shun those who would sacrifice your autonomy beyond what you allow. Create, casting off all guildry and tradition; imitate no prior artist. Achieve the individual, that pure, radiant promise of all liberty; for you alone can matter to yourself. Love cautiously. Enter only into those unions that satisfy but ensure release. Step into no room that lacks an exit; sign no contract without a clause that unsigns. Only thus, only as free, can you succeed.

How can we possibly resist this sound advice? Are these not among the most noble of human sentiments? The lover hears it but not heeds it. The mother will not abandon the ropes that knot her to her child, nor would the

child leave the home to roam unkept. The patriot warrior may fight for freedom but not to be free from his loyalty. The speech is perhaps uneven; but
in hearing it we realize the truth of it—truth itself being a species of the
unfree. At the very least it shows us importantly that the free itself can
deceive, that not all of it is good. To protest that these libertarian excesses
do not represent true freedom is entirely legitimate, but in making the
protest the truth of irony is inescapable. Why, we now ask, provisionally
warned of the dangers in naivete about freedom, is asking threatened by even
this one-sided appeal to liberty? It is now necessary to dig more deeply and
ask what it means to submit to the thrall of fundamental asking.

Submission is the point. The asker, like the lover, the worshiper, the
poet, the patriot, surrenders to the awe. His idol is truth made true in its
being asked, just as the unclad are not naked until they are told. The asker,
as thinker, submits to truth. He does not first have beliefs which then are
tested by supports called reasons, as if reason were a mere crucible—for from
whence did these beliefs themselves first arise? From nonrational resources?
Rather it is the splendid, frightening, even glorious mystery of our own being
that confronts us with the necessity to ask. Who are we that thou are mindful of us? Submission, even to truth, seems inimical to the free. If, however,
we understand the true essence of the great askers, we realize that they glory
in their submission; for what they submit to is the tyranny of truth's love,
which, like uncovered beauty, ensnares our eyes. Even ordinary asking
denudes this meek submission. The scientist, assuming the experiment will
support a developing hypothesis, finds to his momentary chagrin that the
facts rebel against this regime. After several repetitions he is forced to con-
cede the scheme lacks teeth. This is yielding to truth. Even the reluctance to
abandon a heretofore helpful guidance is not as strong as the new, invading
power that changes not the information but what makes the information
intelligible. The suitor asks, and submits either joyously or miserably to the
beloved's response. The author, preparing his characters for the comedy he
wants to write, finds their own authority wreaks a tragedy—as Mark Twain
confesses in his writing *Pudd'nhead Wilson*—and he submits to this integrity
of his own fictionally created characters. It is thus neither ignoble nor misological to recognize authority beyond ourselves; and if it is indeed authority—or even power—why should we not submit to it?

The free and the busy thus render us non-askers. This negative or indirect approach suggests that what enables fundamental asking is at least submission to the existential truth inherent in our own suspension between the
above and the below. The enemies of this submission are the busy and the

free, for both distract from our original power to ask. Yet, the venturing has made it impossible to offer this glibly. It is supremely unsettling to learn the dark ironies that transform the free promise into a bondage of duty, that doing and being oppose each other even as they need each other. The ironies become lures themselves. Perhaps, then, we need further reflection on this central power.

Irony, as is noted in a previous chapter, is originally a figure of speech. Why should this be? What is it that makes irony, as a figure, work? There is no doubt that it does work. Ask a good writer why he uses irony, and he will tell us that it is one of the most powerful tools in his repertoire, even if he is unsure why it is so effective. Ask a great writer why he uses irony and the response is more likely that he does not *use* it. Rather it emerges inevitably, like a hidden truth demanding its presence be honored, suggesting that it lies in the very nature of language itself. In both its Swiftian and tragic senses, the etymology of the term is curious: it is, from the Greek, a speaking against speaking, a turning of language against itself. In Swift, the opposite of what is said is what is meant. In the tragic sense, the opposite of what is "said," that is, represented—such as the nobility of the hero—is countered by what follows dramatically: the ignobility of his end. But even given this etymology, why should speaking against speaking belong so intimately to speaking itself?

One obvious point about tragic irony is the insidious cruelty of fate. We all are fated, of course, but in the tragic hero this being fated is magnified to the point of fascination, thereby becoming a mirror to our own submission to the uncontrolled. It is not fate that enables irony, however; it is irony that enables fate. Just as we must be told we are naked, so we must be told, or shown by art, we are fated. In an earlier work, left unread by millions, called *Why Me?*, I tried to show that fate is possible only in the telling of a story. In the unfolding of the drama or narrative, the free alone can be fated and the fated alone can be free. The reason for this, I suggest in that ill-fated book, is that only those who matter can be free ("mattering" is how we fit into our story); and only the free can matter—where *free* means our possibility to be responsible, without which no story can have meaning. It is only because we can literally "tell" our story that we can live a life. Causal efficacy, conceived as a general principle, accounts for individual events, that may or may not shape our lives, but the coalescence of these events into a nongeneral but still universal authority—the formal notational differences in symbolic logic between generality and universality were pointed out to me by Herman Stark—is provided only in stories that weave the free and the fated into a wearable fabric. Still, it is the success of irony and not the commercial unsuccess of my earlier work, that vindicates the effort. It is not incumbent on us to dig into the authority of our fate; it is enough to realize that one reason for the immense power of irony to make a drama or story accessible is the universal authority it has to mirror our fated reality and hence our ironic asking.

Fate, however, is not the only—or even most important—truth that irony mirrors. Why should a reader find meaning in an ending that mocks what has preceded it? Many stories are hugely satisfying just because they are not ironic; as when a worthy hero, after tribulations and suffering, achieves what he deserves. There is more than mere moral instruction here, as if such tales are told solely to guide the young to good conduct. There is a palpable delight just in hearing Silvius finally and deservedly win his reluctant Phoebe. We cannot gainsay this pleasure, nor should we. If we do take delight in a deserving character achieving a worthy success, then why should we take delight—if that is the right word—when the expectation is thwarted? The thwarting at least has this effect: it transcends what is merely justificatory in storytelling. Perhaps irony appeals just because, in mocking what is earned, the autonomy of the unearned stands out. This, as noted above, emphasizes the existential meaning beyond that of a moral desert, while still leaving the authority of morals intact. Stories that rely too heavily on merit may obfuscate the autonomy of what stories reveal, reducing stories to messages. Even if we accept this suggestion, though helpful, it as yet does not suffice.

Is a warrior's death on the battlefield ironic? On the one hand, it seems not: those who live by the sword die by it. It seems fitting the soldier should die where he himself lived so ardently. On the other hand, we might say it is ironic just because one who lived so long by victory was cheated by defeat. This, too, seems fitting, but only because it is unfitting. We expect past victors to win, not to lose. Their defeat mocks the continuity by bringing it to an end. If the warrior's death by the hand of war is ironic, it is so because it is both fitting and unfitting; or rather, it is fitting because it mocks a certain species of fitness. It mocks that fitness which rests entirely on the level of the earned, and not at all on the level of the telling.

That the telling on its own matters must now be tortured, for the victim on our rack has not yet yielded all his secrets. Our own glibness has abetted the treason. We say that irony either says what is not meant or thwarts the noble by tragic defeat. To say what is not meant is simply lying; to thwart the noble is unjust. We ratchet the rack tighter, then: irony says what is not meant in a way that lets us know what is really meant; the hero is defeated in a way that isolates his worth from the unsuccess of his actions. It is the *way* the deceit is offered that shows it *as* deceit, making it honest. The way in which irony exposes its own deceit is the artful, both in the sense of belonging to art and in the sense of cunning. If we artfully say the opposite of what we mean, then it does not deceive, for the hearer hears not only what is said but the manner in which it is said, and thus learns what is true in the unexpressed possibility lurking within the sham of the actual. This obviously works, that is, we read ironic works successfully. But why the art? Is it not simpler and more honest to say what we mean directly? If I say, "the sun sets in the east," in a sufficiently artful way so that the hearer knows I mean the sun sets in the west, then why take such a torturous route, unless it be for some unworthy pedantry, testing the hearer for his cynicism. Perhaps we should tighten the rack one notch further, for the tortured seems ready yet to confess more.

The truth enabled by irony is not the same as the pre-ironic claim. The tortured now confesses the bareness of his soul. This discovery is of great import, for it shows us the essence of the ironic figure—and perhaps of all of the great figures. But what does it mean? When Antony assures the Roman rabble that Brutus and the others are honorable men, he is not merely saying artfully they are dishonorable; he is also showing that even the genuinely honorable—as Brutus may be—can imperil the magnificent. Perhaps in the presence of a Caesar mere honor is not enough. We must also recognize the meaningfulness of greatness. To suggest ironically that those who put paper in the wrong recycling bin should be shot at dawn is not merely to say they ought not to be shot at dawn, but that even the present modest sanction is yet too severe. More important, ironically to show that the royal raiment belongs to King Lear seeking to strip himself, is more than merely to tell us how important are the regal robes. It also shows the whole specter of civility that comes unraveled when a king is treated as if he wore nothing: "a bare, forked animal." To suggest that an ironic twist at the end of a story enhances the plot by a counter-fittedness overlooks the deeper truth that fate, as the father of the figure, recasts the entire story which now must be read again. Irony therefore does not merely say artfully the opposite of what is meant so that what is meant is gleaned in the hearing. Irony also discovers in the truth of what is meant greater meaning than if it were stated directly.

What do these refinements suggest? At the very least, if irony is a figure of speech, then speech is more than mere propositions. It is a deeply satisfying triumph of language over mere claims or statements. It also suggests there is a profound species of truth reachable only by irony: there is a deeper coherence uncovered only by an incoherence on the propositional level. What beguiles by the cheapening of language in its reduction to claims must be violated violently in order to let us in on the mystery. Only if the banal is rendered incoherent can the profound emerge. To torture our now confessing victim further, we ratchet once again: since irony is a figure of language in art, we realize that to find art in something is to find reason in it. How is this to be accounted?

Theories of tragedy abound like noxious weeds choking out the flowers of the actual dramas. We are asked to study the sayings of Oedipus, Jocasta, Chorus, to ruminate with scholars on what the Greeks thought about fate, and never once asked to consider ourselves as we watch the play. In this these learned deceivers forget what their own erudition tells them: what matters is the audience; and, though this be sacrilege to the antiquarian and relativist alike, it really does not matter if the audience be ancient or our own. It is we the audience for whom the play was written, and so its essence must be found in what *we* discover. Oedipus seeks passionately for truth; his wife seeks just as passionately to keep him from seeking it. It is we in the audience, however, who feel directly, as sharers in the Dionysian mystery, both a loathing and a longing for the truth to emerge. In that art form—which is to say in our own direct, pathoempirical submission to it (for if you leave us out there never *is* an art at all)—we hate, even as we love, truth as it is happening. To hate it and to love it is to let speaking speak against itself. In this we do not use irony as a device, we bare our own ironic essence. Irony "works" because we are ourselves ironic. But now irony is grounded in the existential reality of our own asking. It is not that a Greek hero called Oedipus is seeking after a truth that will destroy him; it is our ability to submit to the deep irony of our own reality: to love and hate truth in a way that alone tells us what being true really means.

To protest that irony is merely a figure of speech is to misunderstand rather grossly the capital importance of language. If we must be told we are naked in order to be naked, and if being naked matters; or if we must be told we are fated in order to be fated, and being fated matters; or if irony is possible only though language and irony matters because truth matters; then perhaps the phrase "merely a figure of speech" is either denuding of appalling ignorance or it is ironic in itself. We need language in order to ask, and asking itself is mattering—at least if it is fundamental asking.

The power of irony to reveal is sometimes forced upon us as an

unwanted discovery. In the suggestion that the busy and the free are impediments to fundamental asking, it was noted that a freely, i.e., morally, made
promise unfrees us, by binding our future. The irony here is palpable: How
can we become more free by becoming less free? Unless I can be morally
responsible, being free means nothing; being responsible seems, however, a
severe check upon my being free. To try to escape the irony by refining definitions is simply dishonest. True, we now realize that the free is not the wanton, that not all indebtedness is a fault, that nobility plays a role in both
freedom and duty. These are all acceptable discoveries; but they do not make
the turmoil any less ironic, for irony is of their essence. It may also be ironic
that suffering, by its nature something we must abhor, is embraced fully by
the lover as an opportunity for sacrifice. Do we, as lovers, desire the beloved
to love as well? If so, and if our own willingness to sacrifice is an important
part of our loving, then it would seem we want our beloved to be able to suffer sacrificially for us. But this seems outrageous. Is it a greater love to
embrace this horrible truth? or to prefer our beloved not to love in return?
So deeply do I love thee I would not have thee love me? Either is painful to
contemplate. Perhaps the busy are wise: perhaps we ought not to ask such
things.

If the busy and the free are inimical to fundamental asking, yet both the
busy and the free reveal truth-revealing ironies of the deepest sort, then perhaps it is the depth itself that matters, so that even these identifications are
suspicious. One must be chary of them, but the paradoxical and the ironic
do not invalidate. Indeed they do not even confuse except on precisely that
level where ready answers eclipse our asking deeply. And so the indirect
approach, asking what disables asking, becomes the direct approach. What
enables fundamental asking is to submit freely—already an irony—to the
power of language to make us naked and fated and responsible and ironic
and mirrored; these revelations are inherent in reflection and reflexivity. The
list is helpful, but the reference to language is essential. What enables asking is language. But asking is a species of language. And so, can we now say
that what enables asking is our asking? As long as this is not glib, it is true
enough. Keeping it from being glib, however, is what matters, and only the
askers can do that.

If nothing else, the contemplation of ironies inevitably reveals the existential phenomenon of ranking; for without ranking, both irony and its formal companion, paradox, remain inconsistencies, and force us to misology
rather than philosophy. Ranking is revealed in the adjective *fundamental*—
unless we rank we cannot weigh one authority against the other. Indeed

without rank there is no authority at all: to be a captain is meaningless without a lieutenant below us to command and a major above us to obey. The
ranks are the palpable, concrete phenomena that enable military authority:
we see in them what authority means. To rank some asking as fundamental
is to realize that some ways of asking outrank others. This ranking, however, since it serves truth, cannot be arbitrary. Yet part of the mystery of asking is how this ranking is discoverable. Once more we realize that the actual
can guide us to what enables it: to its possibility within the actual. We hear
an analysis that suggests that asking how geometry is possible is more fundamental than asking whether it is the product of the mind or the senses.
We hear the suggestion that what it means to think is more fundamental
than what kind of thing a thinking mind might be. We even hear the suggestion that having to be told we are naked comes before we are naked, and
that this dependence on language makes it as true rather than as an arbitrary attitude. In all these analyses the notion of ranking is of crucial importance. Yet, ranking itself is not some deeper or more fundamental power;
the ranking comes after the asking and not before, leaving asking more fundamental than ranking. It is only in asking that its ranks are discovered.
There is no a priori rule or algorithm to designate how to rank asking prior
to asking. This shows something of the mystery of asking, but it is mystery
in a curiously comforting sense. If you will, there is a certain trust in the
experiential, though the term *experiential* is far broader and deeper than that
conceived by empirical epistemologists. Yet, though the power of ranking
may be somewhat mysterious, what the ranks themselves mean are bold and
clear. To take one example from our previous reflections: if it is true that the
free are ironically bound by the responsibility inherent in what it means to
be free, then, any critique, dismissal, or rejection of any restraint on the free
must be independently justified. It is never enough to appeal to some existing restraint and use it as an argument that its presence forfeits being free,
as if "real freedom" were license, or an impossible dream, leading us to the
ridiculous metaphysics that, though we "think" we are free, "actually" we
are all determined. This shows the so-called freedom/determinism debate,
if not grounded in existential asking, is itself a sham, since it assumes a level
of metaphysical profundity that, given the way it is asked, it can never
achieve.

   There is more to the philosophical phenomenon of ranking than the
mere positioning of authority on a formal scale. In the admittedly indulgent
metaphor of torturing what it means to let irony speak on the rack of critical analysis, each tightening of the wheel drove the inquiry deeper. This

metaphor of torturing a truth to reveal its secrets is progressive in the sense that as each stage is reached a further asking emerges. The various ratchings of the torture wheel require what was gleaned before; but it is a descent of asking, not answering. At no stage on the level of torture do we discover what is the fundamental answer. To point out certain stages of this discovery independent of the steps that make up the learning, would remove it from its role in the deepening process. The torture metaphor shows us the process of asking fundamentally; it does not provide us with "final" answers. We can realize that, as the descent proceeds, the deeper insights "outrank" the earlier; but such rank is discovered only in the asking itself, not in some previously established method.

Consider the irony in this: we are asking what enables fundamental asking. What would it mean to describe a vast scheme that purports to *answer* this question? There must be truth in these discoveries, which may in some sense be seen as answers, for it was never suggested that answers do not belong in the asking phenomenon. It is rather that the status or rank of "fundamental" cannot be found in an answer that is ripped out of the asking descent—indeed it cannot be found in any answer at all taken by itself. Truth nonetheless emerges in this ongoing phenomenon, as can be seen in the step-by-step "torture" of how irony confesses truth.

There is no doubt that certain special difficulties emerge when we turn our fundamental asking onto asking itself; for when we do this the gnarls of reflexivity seem to intensify, and the duplicity of mirroring is exacerbated. Yet, though these special difficulties cannot be denied, two things need to be said about them. The first is that inherent in these difficulties is a treasure worth the digging; truth seems more glorious when so deeply mined. The second is that all fundamental asking already is about the asker anyway, and so to find the self-reflective and self-reflexive a necessary part of the inquiry is neither truly surprising nor entirely unfamiliar. Greatness in asking is akin to greatness in art: it may be rare, but its very rarity ironically focuses our attention on monumental achievements in our history, both of art and asking. The rare, being remembered, seem somehow more available than ubiquitous banality which is more easily forgotten. Still, there remain special problems in so direct an approach, not the least of which is that too much focus on the mirrored and the mirroring may distract us from the original. Yet, the counterdanger is even greater: that in seeking to find the original of what is mirrored we forget that mirroring is what enables our access to it.

Mirrors reflect the viewer. This seems so obvious that we dismiss it unheard. It is entirely giddy if, seeking to find out about the malfunctioning flashlight I take a mirror to see if the batteries are in backward. It is better to look directly at what can be seen without a reflector than to look at reflections. We use a mirror only because without it we cannot see ourselves. What does this mean? Consider a shy, vulnerable, gawky teenager stepping out of a shower and suddenly seeing his naked image in a full-length mirror, amazing him. What does he see? To say he sees himself is true but not true enough. Does he see himself as others would see him? Perhaps this is a part of what astonishes him. Perhaps, feeling especially vulnerable he reaches for a towel to hide himself, but then hesitates. We may suggest that he is confronting for the first time his now blooming sexuality; but there is more. He may realize his own hitherto unexpected beauty, though he would never use that term. He also is likely to recognize his own shyness, manifest in that clumsy, awkward, but curiously graceful stance—a deer frozen in the headlights. The shyness and vulnerability reach out to him from the mirror, as if they were part of him just as his fingers are. He may, in rapid oscillation, hate and love the mirror for revealing himself—he may hate and love himself, appearing both alluring and repulsive, frightening him with the possibilities in both, yet thrilling him, too. He is reflected as reflective: he sees his own eyes looking at himself, seeing his own seeing, freighted now with huge existential baggage that nevertheless makes him want to soar beyond himself. It is this last that is so important: he is reflected as reflecting. Is it the mirror that enables the reflection? Surely . . . yet . . .

Perhaps in a fundamental sense it is not the mirror that enables the reflection, but the other way around. It is being reflective that allows mirrors to mirror. To ask about asking is to reflect on our own reflection. We have to be told—or shown as in the case of the youth—we are naked. The telling is a mirror. What is almost impossible for the youth is to see the mirror simply as an optical device; a sheet of glass silvered on the back, functioning according to the rules and principles of optical physics. Is such a device the "real" mirror? Or is shyness unshyly submitted the real mirror? In any event, what is beyond dispute is that truth happens in this reflection, even as we say in a lawyerly way that the image is not the real. True, the image is not the real; but the imaging is; the reflected may not be the real, but the reflecting is. The mirror is always, *as* mirror, and not as silvered glass, a mystery; for in its reflecting we hide as well as show ourselves—and show ourselves as hiding. To ask, Who are we that thou art mindful of us? is to ask for a secret to be given. Part of that secret is the mystery of our own asking. There is truth revealed in the youth's discovery. There is truth reflected in the asking that mirrors our nakedness. But if we must be told or shown we are naked, so we must be asked in order to ask. That we ask this of ourselves is no less revealing than that we see ourselves in our own mirroring. The truth of it is what matters, absolutely.

Index